INTRODUCTION

The core of this book is a 71-page, mimeographed, paper, <u>The Flaw in Deterrence</u>, that I wrote in 1982 to gain entrance to the University of Chicago's political science Ph.D. program. Since I had no word processing equipment then, I wrote it with an IBM Selectric typewriter, and the paper contains a number of typographical errors that I did not have time then to detect and correct. That paper, including its errors, is reproduced here (some errors are indicated, but uncorrected). In turn, the paper was developed from two letters of mine that were published in "Harvard Magazine" (Harvard University's alumni magazine) in its April-May, and July-August, 1982 issues. I wrote the letters as a contribution to a discussion of the probability of accidental nuclear war that "Harvard Magazine" was carrying on at that time. Copies of these letters are in Supplemental Appendix 1 of this book.

Since I wrote the paper, <u>The Flaw in Deterrence</u>, I have elaborated on its main ideas. These elaborations are mainly in showing graphically how large numbers of missiles affect the probability of nuclear accidents. These elaborations are in Supp. Appendix 2, a copy of the leaflet, "The Enola Gay and the Apocalypse Equation."

The central idea behind all of these studies is that, **Probability is a function of time**. This is a fundamental principle, similar to the law of gravity, that is neglected by all of the deterrence strategists whose work is analyzed on pages 16-43 (Examples), of this study. The neglect of this principle I think may destroy the human species. I want everyone to understand this danger, and why, because of it, the thermonuclear arsenals, that are supposed to make deterrence work forever, should be deactivated at once, by all nations, regardless of what other nations do. Antagonistic thermonuclear arsenals spell the end of the human species, not permanent peace. People should be devoting their minds to developing non-lethal, non-violent, means for resolving human conflicts, not to "improving" nuclear, and other, weapons of mass destruction.

Supp. Appendix 4, "The Name of the Game," shows how mathematical probability analysis and game theory (which is a branch of rational choice theory) fit together to prove that unilateral nuclear disarmament is the most rational policy.

Supp. Appendix 5 is a 1986 "Parade Magazine" article by Stanford University professor of electrical engineering Martin Hellman (now emeritus professor), that makes essentially the same argument about the probability of nuclear war as <u>The Flaw in Deterrence</u>.

Bradford Lyttle, 2/11/17

THE FLAW IN DETERRENCE

by

Bradford Lyttle

Published by the
Midwest Pacifist Publishing Center
5729 S. Dorchester Ave.
Chicago, IL 60637
Tel: 773.324.0654
Email: blyttle@igc.org

First edition: July, 1983   500 copies
Second edition: February, 2011   25 copies

CONTENTS

"The universe of data out of which reasonable military decisions have to be made is a vast, chaotic mass of technological, economic, and political facts and predictions. To bring order out of the chaos demands the use of scientific method in systematically exploring and comparing alternative courses of action. When the method is true to its own scientific tenets, it is bound to be more reliable by far than the traditional alternative method, which is to solicit a consensus of essentially intuitive judgements among experienced commanders."

- Bernard Brodie, _Strategy in the Missile Age_

(1)

"Some people appear to be very suspicious of calculations - and correctly so. I have written extensively...on how quantitative analysis can lead either wittingly or unwittingly to error, but that does not mean that non-quantitative analyses are any less misleading. There is another reason for using numbers. The only way in which we can communicate even intuitive notions with any accuracy is to use quantitative measures."

- Herman Kahn, _On Thermonuclear War_ (2)

"The numerical illustrations are intended simply to set out as starkly as possible the essential logic of deterrence; there is no intent to light a torch for the "quantifiability" of the factors involved, which are, of course, highly intangible, unpredictable, unmeasurable, and incommensurable except in an intuitive way. It is worth keeping in mind, however, that decision-makers do have to predict, to measure, and, in some sense, to make incommensurable factors commensurate if they are to reach wise decisions. Although, in practice, the factors cannot be given precise numbers, it is legitimate, for theoretical purposes, to pretend that they can be in order to clarify the logic or method by which they should be weighed and compared. The logic is just as applicable to imprecise quantities as to precise ones; to express it in mathematical terms can provide a useful check on intuitive judgment and may bring to light factors and relationships which judgment would miss."

- Glen H. Snyder, _Deterrence and Defense_

(3)

THE FLAW IN DETERRENCE

by

Bradford Lyttle

"No purpose of government is more central than the protection
of its citizens' physical security."
- Richard Smoke (1)

I. THESIS

The purpose of this paper is to demonstrate that the body of thought known
as "deterrence strategy" includes a false assumption that invalidates it as a
reliable foundation for national policy.

The assumption is that it's possible to repeatedly risk a catastrophic event
without the event becoming probable.

When the demonstration is complete, it will be seen that deterrence, far from
being the safest policy possible, the origin of greatest security for the nation,
is an exceedingly dangerous strategy, one that threatens the existence not only of
the nation as a social unit, but perhaps of world civilization itself.

The heart of the demonstration will be the mathematical probability principle
that if a small risk is repeatedly taken over an extended period, the probability
of the event being risked occurring approaches certainty. Since probability theory can be tricky, and sometimes at first can seem to defy "common sense", it may
be helpful to examine some "everyday" examples of the principle in question.

Suppose that we want to know the probability of an event over an extended
period if we know what that probability is over an interval less than the period. Perhaps the simplest example of this problem is offered by the flipping
of a coin. It's evident that the chance of flipping one "head" in one flip is
½ or .50 or 50%. Also, it's true that flipping a coin several times in no way
changes the 50% probability of flipping a head on each flip. But, what's the
chance of flipping at least one head in two flips? An immediate reaction might
be that it's ½ + ½, or 1, 100%, but a little thought will show that that's incorrect, for we know by experience that we can flip a coin twice and not get a
head.

Another guess might be that the probability is ½ x ½, or ¼. But reflection
shows that that's not the right answer either, for if the chance of flipping at
least one head in one flip is 50%, then the chance of flipping at least one head
in two flips must be greater, not less, than 50%.

These considerations suggest that the chance of flipping at least one head
in two flips must be greater than ½, and less than one. Also, we suspect that
there's a mathematical formula, a probability equation, that will enable us to
exactly calculate that chance.

$$\textcircled{I}$$

The equation is this: $P = 1 - (1-p)^n$ where P is the probability of

flipping at least one head in a sequence of flips, p is the chance of flipping a head in one flip (½ or 50%), and n is the number of flips in the sequence (2). Without engaging in a formal derivation of this equation here (3), a brief analysis of it can give insights into why it "works."

The probability of the event in one interval is p. The expression $(1-p)$

therefore is the probability that the event will <u>not</u> occur in that interval. If we raise $(1-p)$ to the nth power, we are simply multiplying the likelihood that

the event won't happen, by itself, for the number of intervals in the sequence. This gives us the probability that the event <u>won't</u> happen over the sequence. The probability that the event will happen over the sequence is then one minus the probability that it won't happen.

To gain a feeling for this equation and the relationships it represents, let's perform several calculations with different probabilities and sequences. Rather than taking my word that the numbers given in this paper are correct, the reader might perform the calculations him or herself. Any pocket calculator with a ten digit display, and a y^x or x^y, and $\sqrt[x]{y}$ or $\sqrt[y]{x}$, functions will handle the

calculations. I use a Sharp EL-506H; about $25. To start off, let's return to our first problem. What's the chance of flipping at least one head in two flips?

$$P = 50\% = .50$$
$$n = 2$$
$$P = 1 - (1-.50)^2 = 1 - (.5)^2 = 1 - .25 = .75 = 75\%$$

The equation shows that in two flips we have a 75% chance of flipping at least one head.

What's our chance of flipping at least one head in ten flips?

$$P = 50\% = .50$$
$$n = 10$$
$$P = 1 - (1-.50)^{10} = 1 - (.50)^{10} = 1 - .000976 = .999 = 99.9\%$$

The equation shows that in ten flips we have a 99.9% chance of flipping at least one head.

Now let's graduate from a coin, in which p is 50%, to a die (one of a pair of dice). Being a cube, a die has six sides. Therefore, the chance of any given number coming up when we throw the die is 1/6 or .167. Suppose that we want to know the chance of throwing a five in two throws:

$$P = .167$$
$$n = 2$$
$$P = 1 - (1 - .167)^2 = 1 - (.833)^2 = 1 - .69 = .31 = 31\%$$

Let's try ten throws:

$$P = .167$$
$$n = 10$$
$$P = 1 - (1 - .167)^{10} = 1 - (.833)^{10} = 1 - .16 = .84 = 84\%$$

While we're thinking about the chances involved in throwing a die, let's also consider the game of "Russian roulette." In Russian roulette, the players put one bullet into the chamber of a revolver. Each player in turn then spins the chamber, presses the revolver's barrel to his or her head, and pulls the trigger. The player who survives the most turns "wins." Since most revolvers are six-shooters, that is, their chambers hold six bullets, the chances of being shot in any turn are the same as those for throwing a given number with a die. In ten turns, a player would have an 84% chance of being killed.

Finally, let's assume that we are throwing a geometrical solid that has one million sides rather than six. In this case, the chance of throwing a five in one throw is 1/1,000,000 or .000001. The chance of throwing at least one five in 10,000 throws is then:

$$P = .000001$$
$$n = 10,000$$
$$P = 1 - (1 - .000001)^{10,000} = 1 - (.999999)^{10,000} = 1 - .99 = .01 = 1\%$$

If we throw the solid one million times, the chance of getting at least one five is:

$$P = .000001$$
$$n = 1,000,000$$
$$P = 1 - (1 - .000001)^{1,000,000} = 1 - (.999999)^{1,000,000} = 1 - .37 = .63 = 63\%$$

To gain a further sense of the equation, the reader might perform more calculations, choosing p and n to his or her fancy.

These numerical experiments show us how the equation works. A further sense of the equation can be gained by asking, What class of mathematical equations does this equation represent? It's an exponential equation, because of the exponent, or power sign, "n". If plotted on a graph, exponential equations produce curves that approach, but never reach, a certain limit. The equation we've been using can be graphed this way:

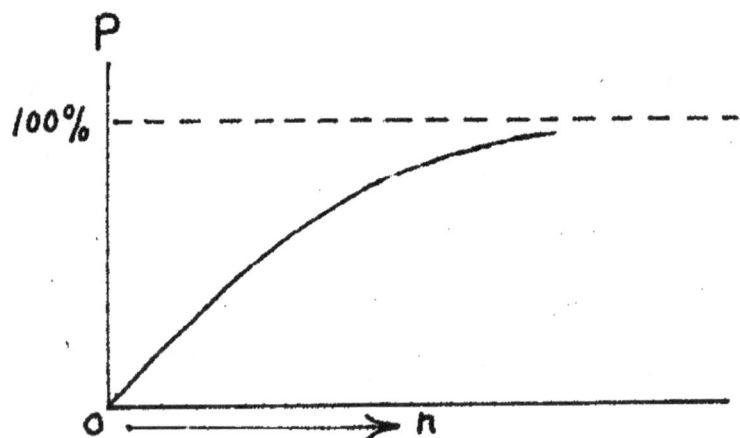

The graph shows that as n increases, the probability of P approaches certainty.

Going back to our coin, we can see how the probabilities produced by different sequences of flips fit this curve. Two flips give a 75% chance of getting a head. Ten flips give a 99.9% chance of seeing at least one head, but even if we flip the coin ten thousand times we'll never get a 100% chance of a head (In 10,000 flips, P = .9999999...%).

With this probability equation and its curve in mind, let's now see if it can be used to gain insights into the failure probability of deterrence.

Deterrence is generally thought of as the policy through which the United States prevents the Soviet Union from attacking us or Western Europe with nuclear weapons. The heart of the policy is a threat we make, to the effect that if we are attacked, we will retaliate in such a way that the Soviet Union will suffer a net loss from its aggression. There is more to deterrence than this. The notion can be applied to situations involving conventional as well as nuclear weapons, and deterrent policies can be employed to try to prevent attacks on parts of the world other than the U.S. and Europe. In all of these situations, the principles are the same. Deterrence involves a threat. The nation that is being threatened refrains from an aggressive action after calculating that losses that will be suffered from the retaliation exceed the possible gains from the attack (4).

For the deterrent threat to be effective, it must be backed up by a means of retaliation, the "hardware." In our time, this consists, primarily, of nuclear weapons arsenals. If a nation makes a threat without possessing the hardware to implement it, then the threat is a bluff, and runs the danger of being understood as such by the "enemy." When the "enemy" realizes that the threat is a bluff, he or she is no longer deterred.

It's evident from these considerations that deterrence depends on creating a certain mental state in the "enemy." Deterrence strategy is primarily speculations about what conditions are necessary to keep the "enemy" convinced that aggressive behavior is unwise. Looked at this way, it appears that with the proper strategy, an appropriate threat, and the right kind of hardware, it should be possible to keep the "enemy" deterred forever. Deterrence strategy therefore becomes an intellectual "balancing" exercise depending on intelligence and knowledge.

None of this thinking involves attempting to apply mathematical probability analysis to the fundamental assumptions of deterrence. Deterrence strategists merely speculate, in the following manner, about the probability that the "enemy" will be deterred by a given strategy: "Because our land-based missiles have become vulnerable to the Soviet Union's SS-20, a "window of vulnerability" has opened, and there's a possibility that the Soviets will attack us. We must close the "window" by installing the invulnerable MX."

The approach of mathematical probability analysis is somewhat different. It asks, "Is there actually a chance that one or more battle-line missiles will be launched, and, if there is, exactly what is the probability in quantitative term?" Answering this question first involves examining several of the basic assumptions of deterrence.

As we've seen, deterrence involves a threat, and the means to implement the threat. The threat's made because U.S. leaders believe that there's a possibility that the Soviet Union will attack the U.S. They seem to believe that this possibility exists because Soviet leaders have expressed hostility toward the U.S., have the nuclear weapons capable of implementing an attack, have expressed contempt for "bourgeois " moral scruples, and have invaded a number of other countries, such as Poland, Finland, Czechoslovakia, Hungary, and Afghanistan. Deterrence is designed to make this possibility of an attack as low as possible. The problem is, if the possibility's assumed at all, the probability equation shows that the probability of an attack will approach certainty. Putting the matter mathematically, in the equation, $P = 1 - (1-p)^n$, if p is greater than zero ($p > 0$) , P will approach certainty. The only way to prevent this is to assume that deterrence can make the probability of an "enemy" attack zero. But this assumption makes deterrence unnecessary, and is never made. In other words, the assumption that makes deterrence necessary, also makes its failure approach certainty.

There's more to the contradiction than this. The threat that makes deterrence "work" involves creating the possibility of an attack. If there was no possibility, the "enemy" wouldn't be deterred. But, as soon as the possibility of an attack is created, the equation shows that the probability of an attack will approach certainty.

Perhaps this second contradiction has never been seen by deterrence strategists because they believe that their side will never attack. For instance, a SAC general might say, "No. There's no possibility that we'll attack the Soviet Union. Our bombers and missiles are only for retaliation." The difficulty with this claim is that it can be made also by the other side for its arsenals. If we take this perspective, there's no chance that either side will attack the other, no matter how large their arsenals may be. In that case, deterrence is unnecessary for anyone.

The arms race testifies to the reality of the situation. Both sides see the arsenals of the other as a threat, as the possibility of an attack. Therefore, they constantly "upgrade" their own arsenals to keep the possibility as low as possible.

Another objection to the anlysis might be that it misrepresents how probability operates. A critic might say, "Well, I agree that there's a chance that the

Soviet Union will attack us, but by keeping the chance very low, we can prevent an attack forever." This criticism fails to recognize that the idea of probability always involves an interval of time. If I say that there's one chance in 50,000 that I'll be hit by a car if I cross the street, I'm saying that during the time it takes me to cross the street there's a one-in-50,000 chance of being hit by a car. It makes no sense to say that the chance of being hit is independent of time, for, if it were, it wouldn't make any difference how many times I crossed the street.

Deterrence strategists seem always to make the mistake of not recognizing that risk is related to time.

The mistake is natural unless one is conscious of mathematical probability theory. A substantial amount of our thinking is involved in trying to minimize risks for ourselves. However, we don't think of it as minimizing risks, we think of it as eliminating risks. For example, we say, "If I put on this sweater, I won't get cold." Or, "If I put gas in my car's tank I won't stall on the expressway." The reality is that by doing these things we reduce or minimize the probability of the unwanted experience. Because in our lifetimes we may never have had the experience, we assume that our actions make its probability zero. The mistake in thinking isn't serious because the unwanted experience isn't very important. Section II of this paper will show how the mistake involves a philosophic error. If made in regard to deterrence, its consequences can be disastrous.

Insights concerning when deterrence will fail

What we've been considering is the probability of the breakdown of strategic deterrence, the likelihood that the highest authorities on one side or the other will decide to attack. This kind of breakdown can be called "an authorized missile launch." However, there's another way that war could break out, and that's by the unauthorized launching of missiles by one side or the other. An unauthorized launch could occur because of a mechanical or electrical breakdown in a launch mechanism, the psychological instability of missile base crews, or mistakes and psychological instabilities on the part of personnel in strategic command centers. Unauthorized launches are a more precise way of describing what's popularly called "accidental war." (6) Some people believe that the unauthorized launch of a missile inevitably would trigger a full-scale general nuclear war. Others believe that by means of the "hot line," and other communication devices between the superpowers, an unauthorized launch could be prevented from resulting in general war. Whatever the true probabilities of the situation may be, everyone would agree that any unauthorized launch could be extremely destructive, and could have very dangerous implications. Once launched, battle-line missiles can't be destroyed or "aborted" in flight (7), and anti-ballistic missile (ABM) systems to intercept them either don't exist (8), or have a low probability of effectiveness. Furthermore, most strategic missiles have more than one warhead; they may have ten. Therefore, the unauthorized launch of even one missile could destroy many important centers in one of the superpowers. The unauthorized launch of a salvo of missiles, say the 15 Minuteman missiles from one base, or the 24 missiles from one Trident submarine, could devastate a country.

In addition, unauthorized launches could "decapitate" a nation's command system, and thus make it very difficult for hot-line restraints to work (9). Under some circumstances, they could be as destructive as authorized launches.

Mathematical probability analysis provides somewhat different insights when applied to authorizied and unauthorized launches, and therefore will be discussed separately.

Authorized launches

What's the probability of an authorized launch? Consider the bipolar U.S./Soviet deterrence relationship. As we've seen, there's always some chance that one side or the other will attack. During any given interval, this chance will be different for each country, but we can combine the two chances into an average chance of some attack during that interval. We can then let the letter p stand for this average chance of some attack, and let our interval be 24 hours, or one day.

Consider now the probability equation: $P = 1-(1-p)^n$. If we want to know p's value, we must re-arrange the equation so that p is the dependent variable, and P one of the independent variables. We can do this in this way:

$$P = 1-(1-p)^n$$
$$-(1-p)^n = P-1$$
$$(1-p)^n = 1-P$$
$$1-p = \sqrt[n]{1-P}$$
$$-p = \sqrt[n]{1-P} -1$$
$$\text{(II)} \quad p = 1-\sqrt[n]{1-P}$$

Given this equation, if we want to know p's value, we must have values for n and P. A key bit of information that enables us to set values for n and P is that no nuclear attack has taken place since bipolar nuclear arsenals have come into existence. Nuclear arsenals have been operational for about 34 years. To simplify our calculations, let's round this off to 30 years. Thirty years is 10,950 days. Therefore, n=10,950.

The independent variable P is the probability of an attack in 30 years. Since no attack has occurred, we can assume that P has been less than probable. Therefore, we can let P=49%, or .49.

Now, we are prepared to calculate p:

$$n = 10,950$$
$$P = .49$$
$$p = 1 - \sqrt[10,950]{1-.49} = 1 - \sqrt[10,950]{.51} = 1 - .99994 = .00006 = .006\%$$

These calculations show that since bipolar deterrence came into effect, the average daily chance of a U.S. or Soviet attack has been no higher than six one thousandths of one percent. It can't have been much higher than this, or an attack would have become probable. I could be lower.

This insight concerning the probability of an attack has several implications. First, it shows that for deterrence tohaveworked as long as it has, the probability of an attack must have been kept very low. That means that both the U.S. and the Soviet Union must have been remarkably restrained and peaceful in their actual attitudes toward each other. This belies the picture of bellicosity painted by aggressive extremists of both sides, who often suggest that one side or the other is itching to attack. It's encouraging to realize that despite their often hard language toward each other, the leaders of both the U.S. and the Soviet Union have been trying to keep matters from getting out of hand.

Another implication is that we can't expect deterrence to work for a long time if we permit p's value to climb to any degree. For example, we can't take high risks with deterrence and expect it to keep on "working."

To illustrate this last principle, let's assume a series of international crises, like the Cuban missile crisis, in which the probability of an attack is high. Let's say that in crisis #1, the probability of an attack is 40%, in crisis #2 it's 20%, in crisis #3, it's 50%. We can calculate the probability of an attack over the three crisis period in this manner:

$$P = 1 - (1-.40)(1-.20)(1-.50)$$
$$P = 1 - (.60)(.80)(.50)$$
$$P = 1 - .24 = .76 = 76\%$$

The calculations show that we probably wouldn't have survived the three crises.

It should be pointed out before summarizing these points, that the approach can apply to deterrence situations with any number of "poles," such as uni-polar, or multi-polar deterrence. In any case, it shows us what the daily probability of an attack has been. Thus, the nuclear arsenals of Great Britain, France, China, India, etc. could be included in the analysis.

To summarize what we now know about the failure probability of strategic deterrence:

1. It approaches certainty;

2. For any given day, it must have been no more than .006% for bipolar deterrence to have "worked" for 30 years;

3. Leaders of both the U.S. and the Soviet Union have shown great restraint. They haven't often seriously considered attacking;

4. The daily strategic launch probability already is so low that severe international tensions easily could make a launch probable;

5. It's impossible to run repeated high risks with deterrence without incurring a high probability of catastrophe.

Unauthorized launches

An analysis of the probability of unauthorized launches, similar to the one that we've just applied to authorized launches, can yield additional insights.

First, it's unnecessary to closely examine the assumptions at the foundation of deterrence strategy to realize that the probability of an unauthorized missile launch is greater than zero. We know that once a missile is battle-ready, it could be launched in a variety of unauthorized ways. Therefore, an unauthorized missile launch will become probable.

Once this is established, there are a variety of other insights about unauthorized launches that can be gained through probability analysis, among them, the upper limit to the probability that any given missile will be launched on any given day, and when it's probable that a missile will be launched.

In regard to the launch probability for any given missile, we can use an analysis similar to that which we employed while investigating authorized launches. The main difference is that when investigating unauthorized launches, the variable that most interests us is the chance of a single missile launch rather than that of a strategic salvo. What is the probability of the unauthorized launch of a single missile?

We can begin the analysis by letting p stand for the probability that any given missile will be launched on any given day (over any 24-hour period). There are many missiles, which means that the chance of at least one of the total number of missiles being launched is greater than the chance of just one missile being launched. If we let m stand for the total number of missiles, the equation that gives us the probability of some missile being launched over the extended period is:

$$\text{(III)} \quad P = 1 - (1-p)^{nm} \quad (10)$$

We are most interested in the value of p. Solving the equation for p, we get:

$$\text{(IV)} \quad p = 1 - \sqrt[nm]{1-P}$$

What are the probable values of our independent variables? We know that together, the U.S. and Soviet Union have about 4,000 strategic missiles; m=4,000.

Also, we know that these missiles have been battle-ready for at least ten years; n=3,650.

Since no missile has been fired, we can assume that P is probably no larger than 49% (.49). So:

$$P = 1 - \sqrt[3,650 \times 4,000]{1-.49} = 1 - \sqrt[14,600,000]{.51} = 1 - .9999999$$

$$= .0000001 = \frac{1}{10,000,000} = 10^{-7}$$

From these calculations, we see that the probability of an unauthorized missile launch cannot have been greater than about one chance in ten million for the likelihood of a launch to have remained improbable over the past decade. This is a very low probability. It suggests that efforts to further reduce the probability of an accidental attack may have little effect, particularly when we consider that few quantified insights exist regarding how any safety measures actually affect the probability of a launch.

When will a launch become probable ? Answering this question by means of a direct mathematical approach requires solving our equation for n:

$$P = 1 - (1-p)^{nm}$$

$$(1-p)^{nm} = 1 - P$$

$$nm = \frac{\log(1-P)}{\log(1-p)}$$

$$\text{(Y)} \quad n = \frac{\log(1-P)}{m \cdot \log(1-p)}$$

In examining equation (Y), it's evident that we know the values of all of the independent variables except p. The value of P is 51% (.51). The value of m is 4,000. In regard to p's value, our first investigation showed that p must be very small, no greater than one chance in ten million (10^{-7}), but it could be smaller than 10^{-7}.

One thing we definitely know about p's value is that p has some definite value. That is, there's a real, rather than an imaginary probability that a given missile will be launched on any given day. This means that there's a date in the future when a missile launch will become probable. Because of the potentially catastrophic consequences of such a launch, I've called the equations that have to do with the calculation of unauthorized launch probabilities "Apocalypse Equations" (11).

While it would be interesting to establish p's real value, and thereby be able to approximate the date of an Apocalyptic nuclear weapons accident, there's no way to do this except by statistically analyzing the failure probabilities of all of the mechanical, electrical, and human systems that control missile launches. While this is technically possible, it's also enormously complicated and expensive. (12).

Despite these considerations, it's thought provoking to realize that if we assume that p is as small as 10^{-8} (one chance in one-hundred-million) a missile launch will become probable within 50 years:

$$n = 18,250$$
$$p = 10^{-8}$$
$$m = 4,000$$
$$P = 1 - (1-10^{-8})^{18,250 \times 4,000} = 1 - (.99999999)^{73,000,000} = 1 - .48 = 52\%$$

Another insight provided by the Apocalypse Equations is that the more missiles there are, the sooner one of them will be fired. This is because m, the number of missiles, is an exponential factor, as shown by equation $P = 1-(1-p)^{nm}$. Increasing or decreasing m will vary the slope of the curve generated by the equation. This can be shown graphically in this way:

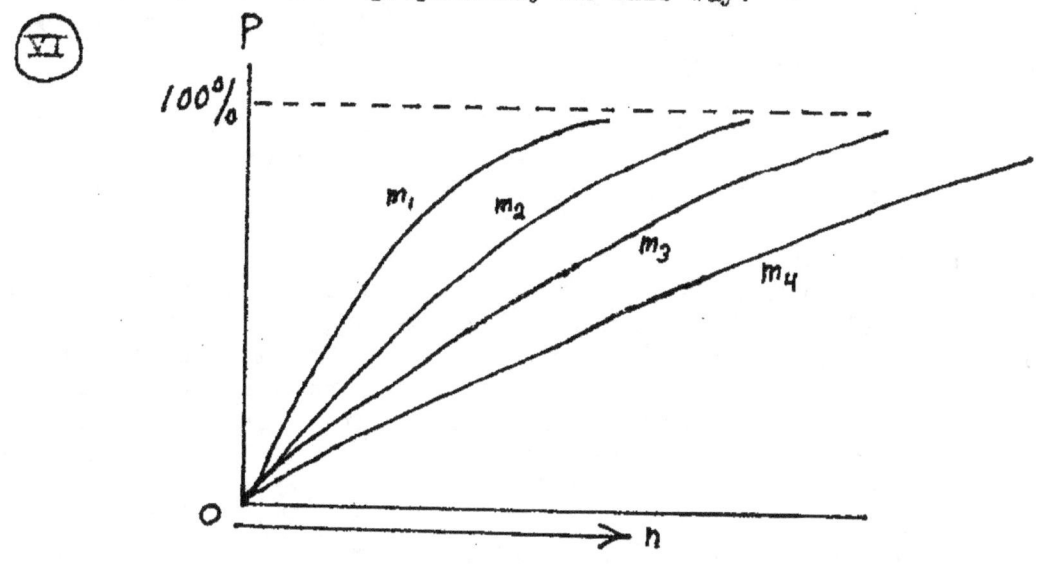

In the graph, $m_1 > m_2 > m_3 > m_4$ (13).

The direct relationship that the number of missiles has to the probability of an unauthorized launch is neglected by deterrence strategists, who hold that large numbers of missiles on both sides invariably help to produce "stable" deterrence systems.

To summarize what we now know about the probability of an unauthorized missile launch:

1. It approaches certainty;

2. It's upper limit can be no more than about 10^{-7} , a value so low that efforts to improve the "safety" of missile systems may have little effect;

3. The probability of an unauthorized launch has a real value that could be approximated by statistical analysis. This means that it's possible to approximate when an unauthorized missile launch will occur;

4. If it's assumed that the probability of a given missile being launched over any 24-hour period is 10^{-8}, a launch becomes probable within 50 years;

5. The more missiles there are, the sooner an unauthorized launch is likely to occur.

While we've separated the analysis into two parts, authorized and unauthorized missile launches, it should be remembered that actually, the probability of a missile launch at any given moment is a combination of the two factors. Since the unauthorized launch factors are stable and quantifiable, we could consider them base factors. The factors related to authorized launches then would be added to these. The added factors might fluctuate considerably as international tensions varied.

In addition, the argument that establishes an unauthorized launch probability for one missile eventually leads to a proof of an unauthorized launch probability for a salvo. If there's an unauthorized launch probability for one missile, there's a probability for two missiles, ten missiles, the missiles in a Minuteman base, in a Polaris submarine; the entire arsenal. Since at some point unauthorized launches would equal strategic salvos in destructive power, there's little practical difference between the two.

We've already seen that the more missiles there are, the greater is the likelihood of an unauthorized launch. What effect has the number of missiles on the probability of an authorized launch?

This question is one of the main issues of conventional deterrence strategy, which, as we've seen, is primarily a body of speculations about how an "enemy's" mental state will be affected by different kinds of threats. Most strategists have come to the conclusion that a "stable" deterrence system, one in which no one will be strongly tempted to launch an attack, will have several characteristics, one of which is large numbers of missiles. Large numbers of accurate missiles, based in ways that would make them difficult to destroy, would insure that a substantial part of a deterrence force could survive a surprise attack, and be able to retaliate effectively against a variety of "enemy" targets. This is one of the main reasons why strategic missile systems have grown so large. The main question isn't whether or not a missile force would be able to destroy the cities of an "enemy." A handful of missiles could do that. The most important question is, How many missiles would have survived a surprise attack, and be able to effectively retaliate? Since surprise attacks can be devastating, it's necessary to have large numbers of missiles to insure the survival of a necessary minimum for retaliation. Large numbers of missiles helps to make deterrence "credible."

This last insight provides us with the ability to see what deterrence really means for the United States and world civilization. Conventional deterrence strategy has brought into existence huge arsenals of very accurate, well protected nuclear missiles that have the capacity for quickly obliterating civilization as we know it. The view that these arsenals can compose a stable deterrence system, and the missiles will never be deliberately launched in a strategic attack, is an illusion. Probability analysis shows that the probability of a strategic attack approaches certainty. In addition, the analysis shows that the probability of unauthorized missile launches also approaches certainty, and that this probability will increase as the number of missiles increases. These facts mean that deterrence, far from being a wise national policy that can insure national security, is about the most dangerous policy that can be conceived within the present scientific and technological state of civilization.

Deterrence can be considered irrational partly because it inexorably tends to generate a catastrophe - a nuclear war that could destroy civilization and perhaps the human species - which is greater than the catastrophe it's intended to prevent.

II. A PHILOSOPHIC ERROR

Before analyzing the works of various deterrence strategists to see if they've taken into consideration mathematical probability analysis, I'd like to explain a philosophic error that frequently crops up in deterrence strategy. As we've seen, deterrence strategy is largely speculation about psychological states, how various configurations of weapons will affect an "enemy's" inclination to attack. Once a strategic model has been created, discussed, adopted as national policy, and given expression in hardware, strategists have tended to evaluate it entirely on the basis of whether or not it's "worked." Since no battle-line nuclear bombs have been exploded since 1945, strategists naturally have come to the conclusion that deterrence has worked. From that belief, it's an easy step to the conviction that deterrence will continue to work. A concise way of putting this view is that, "Deterrence will work because it has worked."

That way of making predictions about policies is natural. It's based on the assumption that patterns that can be detected in the past will be repeated in the future. Such an assumption underlies most of our conscious behavior. We've learned how to act in the world by thinking about our experiences, our personal history. A child refrains from putting his or her finger into a fascinating candle flame because he or she remembers the pain that resulted from the first exploration. An adult may put on a woolen sweater before going jogging, because he or she remembers how unpleasant it was to jog in the cold of the day before. As a rule of thumb, believing that what's happened in the past will occur in the future is a wise way of approaching life. It's called "learning from experience."

But, as an iron-clad rule, it's risky. It shoudn't always be considered the most reliable way for predicting the future. This is because it involves what philosophers call the error of "induction." Induction involves establishing the likelihood of an event in the future by noting that the event has occurred in the past. Philosophers point out that although it's natural to believe that patterns of past events will repeat themselves, there's no <u>logical</u> reason why they should. (1)

Patterns repeat themselves because of reasons, conditions, not because of logic. If the conditions change, the patterns may not be repeated. A simple example of this is the driver of a car who expects the car to stop when he or she puts his or her foot on the brake. The expectation is rooted in past experience, which, in turn, depends on the car's brake system being mechanically sound. If a brake line rusts through and allows brake fluid to leak out, the driver may be unpleasantly surprised when he or she depresses the brake pedal on coming to an intersection.

Because of this, it's simply not philosophically sound to proclaim that, "Deterrence will work because it always has worked," or that, "Deterrence has worked for thirty years, therefore it will continue to work." Conditions may change, or probability factors may be operating of which we're unaware.

III. A THEORY OF HISTORY

The probability equations and the curves they generate provide insights regarding history. Historians often have noted that history seems mainly a record or wars, and the rise and decline of nations. Wars imply competitive arsenals, and competitive arsenals imply military strategy - deterrence strategy (1). A study of political thought will show that concepts of deterrence always have preoccupied national leaders. They've been interested in presenting so strong a face to "enemies" that the "enemies" won't attack. Yet, wars have repeatedly occurred. The reason is that the deterrence strategies have been inherently unstable, governed by the probability equation, $P = 1-(1-p)^n$. "Peace" is that period during which war is improbable , or less than 50%. "War" has occurred when time has extended to produce a period within which war's probability is high, more than 50%. Statesmen and historical philosophers (2) have been perplexed by their inability to prevent war, and by the complexity and subtlety of the factors that have precipitated war. Actually, the key to the problem hasn't been in the maze of factors, it's been in the mathematical probability laws that govern deterrence. Given deterrence and enough time, the outbreak of war became probable, no matter how skillfully different factors were juggled.

At different times in history, different nations have been powerful. These nations have expanded until blocked by other nations. The expansion can be seen as the rapid failure of deterrence strategies. When the expanding nation encountered an opponent of nearly equal power, it has taken more time for the deterrence policies to fail.

History can be represented by a graphic model showing this repeated failure of deterrence:

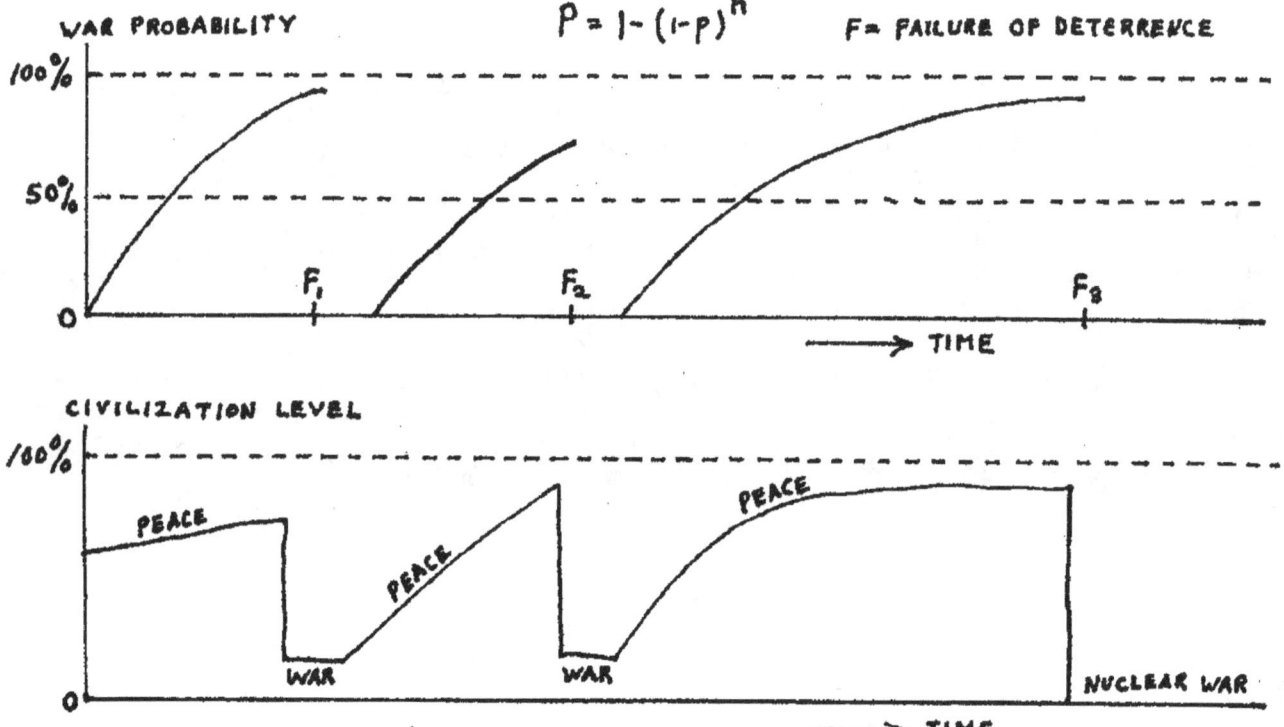

I call the last wave "The death curve of civilization."

This interpretation of history suggests that the theory of a "balance of power" has never been valid. "Balancing power" by means of arms buildups and the formation of alliances hasn't created peace, it's only postponed war by driving the variable p to a low level.

Likewise, the phrase, "*si vis pacem, para bellum*," "if you wish peace, prepare for war," is exposed as a dangerous deception. Preparing for war can't guarantee permanent peace, it can only postpone war.

The durability of nations hasn't been due to their ability to avert war, it's been the result of their ability to win wars, or not be dismembered if they lose. The United States has never enjoyed more than a decade or two of peace. It's geographic advantages, and democratic political system, have been main factors in enabling it to win all of the major wars it's fought. It's difficult to see how the U.S or the Soviet Union will "win" the nuclear war implied ultimately by nuclear deterrence and the probability equations.

IV. EXAMPLES

This section is made up of analyses of important writings of influential deterrence strategists. It will show that none of these strategists has been aware of the implications of mathematical probability analysis for deterrence strategy. All believe that nuclear war can be repeatedly risked without war becoming probable . Also, they've been unaware of the philosophic pitfalls inherent in induction. Section IV will show how these oversights have led strategists into many erroneous beliefs that have dangerous policy implications. The order of the analyses is roughly chronological in reference to the works being considered.

John Foster Dulles

Although John Foster Dulles usually may not be thought of as a deterrence strategist, he was one of the first. He coined the phrase "massive retaliation". Defending his Indochina policies in a January, 1956 Life magazine article, he suggested the notion of "brinksmanship":

"You have to take chances for peace, just as you must take chances in war...Some say that we were brought to the verge of war. Of course we were brought to the verge of war. The ability to get to the verge without getting into war is the necessary art. If you cannot master it, you inevitably get into war. If you try to run away from it, if you are scared to go to the brink, you a lost. We've had to look it square in the face - on the question of enlarging the Korean war, on the question of getting into the Indochina war, on the question of Formosa. We walked to the brink and we looked it in the face. We took strong action." (1)

A cover-page note calling attention to the story said, "Three Times at Brink of War: How Dulles Gambled and Won: (2). The note and story deeply frightened many people, who could easily see that it was impossible safely to take repeated large risks. Adlai Stevenson accused Dulles of playing "Russian roulette" with world peace.

It's clear that Dulles had no understanding of probability theory, or even intuition of its most general principles. He believed in "manipulating risk." Adlai Stevenson had an intuitive sense of probability theory, but apparently didn't realize that the "Russian roulette" principle was imbedded in all deterrence strategies.

Henry A. Kissinger

The main theme of Henry Kissinger's Nuclear Weapons and Foreign Policy (1957) (3) is that the United States must develop a capacity for limited war, including limited nuclear war as well as conventional war, if its deterrence posture is to remain credible. Kissinger traces the development of atomic weapons, maintains that their destructiveness has revolutionized warfare, points out that the greatest danger today can be from a nuclear surprise attack, since such an attack could be decisive, and maintains that the emphasis that the U.S. has placed on strategic nuclear forces has tended to paralyze policy. If the only response to every "enemy" maneuvre is a threat to unleash all out nuclear war, such threats soon will become meaningless. Kissinger argues that the U.S. should develop tactical nuclear forces, and strengthen its conventional ones. In addition, he argues for strong leadership that can seize opportunities, and won't be bound by the time-consuming processes of "committees."

Kissinger expresses no understanding of probability theory. He accepts the idea that deterrence depends upon the manipulation of risk, but doesn't realize that such a policy makes war probable. For example, here he is discussing the deterrent effects of a Soviet ballistic missile submarine fleet:

"...Submarines with 1,500-mile missiles will in effect be able to place any island under siege and threaten portions of the globe which are now immune to Soviet attack, such as Australia. They will add considerably to the Soviet strategic striking power even against the continental United States. Over 50 per cent of the population of the United States lives within three hundred miles of the coastline. Submarines with 1,500-mile missiles lying 500 miles off-shore could cause fearful damage. To be sure, such an attack could not prevent our launching a devastating counterblow against the U.S.S.R. and would therefore not enable the Soviet Union to win an all-out war. But it will be an additional form of blackmail. It will increase the reluctance of the free world to run the risks of an all-out war and may thereby paralyze resistance to aggression short of a direct onslaught on the United States." (4)

The paragraph suggests that Kissinger accepts "brinksmanship" as a continuous, national policy. This impression is reinforced by the following paragraph. Kissinger wants to make "a strategy of limited war stick" by being willing to risk "Armageddon" :

"Even among the major powers the strategy outlined in this chapter will not be easy to implement. It presupposes a military capability which is truly graduated. It assumes a diplomacy which can keep each conflict from being considered the prelude to a final showdown. Above all, it requires strong nerves. We can make a strategy of limited war stick only if we leave no doubt about our readiness and our ability to face a final showdown. Its effectiveness will depend on our willingness to face up to the risks of Armageddon." (5)

In The Necessity for Choice (1960) (6), Kissinger revises and expands many of the positions he expressed in Nuclear Weapons and Foreign Policy. In regard to limited war, he acknowledges the growing body of opinion that it would be extremely difficult to keep any nuclear conflict limited, and any nuclear war would devastate the area where it was fought. He shifts from discussing strategy in terms of preparing for limited nuclear wars, to proposing ways in which conventional forces can be strengthened and backed-up with nuclear ones to maintain a strong deterrence posture, and increase the likelihood that war, if it occurs, will remain conventional.

Recognizing the dangers of the arms race, he discusses disarmament and arms control. Much of his analysis is noteworthy because its principles and arguments can be found in most of today's deterrence strategy, and even has spilled over into the position of the nuclear weapons freeze campaign. For example, Kissinger argues that deterrence systems with fairly large numbers - hundreds - of well-hardened missiles would be more "stable" than complete nuclear disarmament, or deterrence systems with only a few dozen missiles. Large well hardened arsenals are more difficult to destroy in surprise attacks, hence help to insure a retaliatory capacity. Small arsenals could be wiped out easily, and both small arsenals and zero nuclear weapons situations could be completely "destabilized" by small, clandestine caches of nuclear weapons. Kissinger writes:

"The discussion about nuclear disarmament has revealed the paradoxical fact that there is a certain safety in numbers. And this is true even if both sides scrupulously observe an agreement to limit nuclear weapons or the means of delivery. Instability is greater if each side possesses 10 missiles than if the equilibrium is stabilized at, say, 500. For an attack which is 90 per cent successful when the defender has 10 missiles leaves him one - or a number hardly likely to inflict unacceptable damage. An attack of similar effectiveness when the defender possesses 500 missiles leaves 50 - perhaps sufficient to pose an unacceptable risk in retaliation. And of course it is technically more complicated to destroy such a large number. Reduction of numbers is thus not an infallible remedy. A very small and vulnerable retaliatory force may increase the danger of war by encouraging the opponent to risk surprise attack...

If the permissible number of long-range delivery vehicles is set at zero - if, in other words, both sides agreed to destroy all ICBM's and nuclear weapons - even a small evasion, say ten hidden missiles or airplanes, will confer a decisive advantage. And such an evasion is almost impossible to discover. If the number is set very low, say at 10, an additional 15 may make a surprise attack possible. In such circumstances, there would be a dual incentive for evasions: fear of the opponent's evasion and the temptation to deal with the security problem once and for all by launching a surprise attack.

On the other hand, if the number is set relatively high, say at 500, even a fairly substantial violation would not confer a decisive advantage. In that case, 50 additional long-range missiles or airplanes would not enable the violator to launch a surprise attack. A decisive advantage can be obtained only by so many weapons that the risk of detection is likely to appear excessive." (7)

As was pointed out in Part I of this paper, the difficulty with this position is that it ignores mathematical probability theory. When the probability of a missile launch approaches certainty, even with the most "balanced" strategic forces , the existence of large arsenals simply insures catastrophic destruction for everyone.

At the end of <u>Nuclear Weapons and Foreign Policy</u>, Kissinger describes his idea of political leadership in the nuclear age. In a lengthy analysis of communist ideology, he comes to the conclusion that the rather simple, rigid character of Marxist/Leninist thought makes it easier for communist leaders to arrive at strategic decisions, than it is for statesmen in the West, who tend to have a pragmatic, more scientific viewpoint, that withholds decisions until "all of the facts are in." Consequently, Western statesmen may be unable to seize opportunities, and may be left behind in the struggle for strategic advantage.

"...Policy is the art of weighing probabilities; mastery of it lies in (in) grasping the nuances of possibilities. [How true!] To attempt to conduct it as a science must lead to rigidity. For only the risks are certain; the opportunities are conjectural. One cannot be "sure" about the implications of events until they have happened and when they have occurred it is too late to do anything about them. Empiricism in foreign policy leads to a penchant for *ad hoc* solutions. The rejection of dogmatism inclines our policy-makers to postpone committing themselves until all facts are in; but by the time the facts are in, a crisis has usually developed or an opportunity has passed. Our policy is, therefore, geared to dealing with emergencies; it finds difficulty in developing the long-range program that might forestall them." (8)

Kissinger pursues this theme to the end of the book. He concludes:

"...we should be able to leaven our empiricism with a sense of urgency. And while our history may leave us not well enough prepared to deal with tragedy, it does teach us that great achievement does not result from a quest for safety. Even so, our task will remain psychologically more complex than that of the Kremlin. As the strongest and perhaps the most vital power of the free world we face the challenge of demonstrating that democracy is able to find the moral certainty to act without the support of fanaticism and to run risks without a guarantee of success." (9)

Since Kissinger is unaware that repeatedly running risks, and facing Armageddon, will make nuclear war probable, he has consistently, if unconsciously, carried out this vision of statesmanship in his own governmental career. Quite the opposite to a "guarantee of success" in the risks he has unfanatically run, is the guarantee of probable catastrophic failure. Kissinger's career can be regarded as a quest for national security that's been conducted without an essential analytical   tool: an understanding of mathematical probability theory.

Albert Wohlstetter

One of the most frequently cited works in deterrence literature is Albert Wohlstetter's article, "The Delicate Balance of Terror," that was published in the January, 1959 edition of Foreign Affairs (10). The article is a comprehensive, yet compact summary of deterrence issues that were considered critical at the time, and the positions that Wohlstetter advocates may be considered spiritual as well as practical guidelines for the subsequent development of deterrence strategy in this country. Major points that he makes are:

- Deterrence depends on a second strike rather than a first-strike capability. For this reason, simply having nuclear weapons and the means to deliver them isn't enough. It's necessary to have an arsenal that can survive a surprise attack, and be delivered to its target;

- It isn't easy to maintain a credible retaliatory capacity. Many factors, including the possible loss of command centers and communications, and enemy defenses, could make very difficult effective retaliation;

- There's no alternative to deterrence. Since small caches of nuclear weapons always could be concealed, safe, inspected disarmament is impossible;

- The U.S. has the intellectual and spiritual resources to maintain an effective deterrence posture.

Nowhere in the article is there any evidence that Wohlstetter understands mathematical probability theory. For example, he writes, "Deterrence is a matter of comparative risks...Deterrence will require an urgent and continuing effort." (11) In terms of the probability equation, the notion of continuing risks can only have meaning if $p > 0$.

Wohlstetter apparently believes that deterrence can be maintained indefinitely by the exertion of sufficient intellectual and spiritual energy. In the paragraph that concludes the article, he writes:

"A generally useful way of concluding a grim argument...would be to affirm that we have the resources, intelligence and courage to make the correct decisions. That is, of course, the case. And there is a good chance that we will do so. But perhaps, as a small aid toward making such decisions more likely, we should contemplate the possibility that they may not be made. They are hard, do involve sacrifice, are affected by great uncertainties and concern matters in which much is altogether unknown and much else must be hedged by secrecy; and above all, they entail a new image of ourselves in a world of persistent danger. It is by no means certain that we shall meet the test." (12)

Mathematical probability analysis shows that no matter how much intelligence, energy, and courage are expended on deterrence, in a world of persistent danger, the probability that the "tests" won't be met approaches certainty.

Perhaps the title of the article is the most striking example of Wohlstetter's lack of awareness of mathematical probability theory. What makes a balance "delicate"? Surely, the high possibility at any given moment that it will upset. Therefore, the probability that a delicate balance will be upset rapidly approaches certainty.

Bernard Brodie

Bernard Brodie's book, Strategy in the Missile Age (13), is considered one of the seminal works on deterrence. The main theme of the book is that nuclear, particularly thermonuclear weapons, have drastically changed the nature or warfare. While in pre-nuclear times a society could be actively protected against destruction during warfare, in the nuclear age this no longer is true. Therefore, what's most important is to prevent nuclear war. This best can be done by deterrence. Brodie argues that deterrence requires a "rational enemy," who weighs the gains and costs of every situation, and decides not to attack as long as the costs exceed the gains. For this reason, deterrence depends on having a reliable second-strike capability. Brodie recognizes that carrying out retaliation in the event that deterrence fails can be considered irrational and vindictive.

Many passages in the book show that Brodie is unaware of the mathematical probability factors that affect the success of deterrence. For example, in writing about the ultimate philosophical justification for deterrence, he writes;

"...there are some things which we want very much (for example, national integrity and independence) and which we do not know how to defend against external menace except by threatening certain actions which do risk national suicide. We justify or rationalize this posture on the ground that our threats will suffice to hold the menace in check and will not be challenged." (14)

In the following passage, he writes that stable deterrence can be maintained over "the long term":

"Deterrence after all depends on a subjective feeling which we are trying to create in the opponent's mind, a feeling compounded of respect and fear, and we have to ask ourselves whether it is not possible to overshoot the mark. It is possible to make him fear us too much, especially if what we make him fear is our over-readiness to react, whether or not he translates it into clear evidence of our aggressive intent. The effective operation of deterrence over the long term requires that the other party be willing to live with our possession of the capability upon which it rests." (15)

In both passages, Brodie assumes that it's possible to continue to take risks indefinitely without facing the growing likelihood of nuclear war.

In Brodie's article, "On the Objectives of Arms Control," (16) there are other passages which show that he isn't aware of probability theory. Here, he writes about a "probability of war" continuing to be extremely low:

"I find the Kahn-Weiner statement provocative because of their view of priorities. My own contrary view is that in a pragmatic approach to arms control the object of saving money really deserves a superior rating to that of saving the world. The conclusion must imply, among other things, either a high confidence that the probability of war between the two superpowers will continue to be extremely low, or the conviction that in any case we cannot do much about that probability through arms control. To make explicit and thus also to clarify what is otherwise ambiguous, let me record that I subscribe to both propositions." (17)

In this passage, he expresses puzzlement over why arms races lead to war:

"...Why the pressures of an arms competition, however costly, irritating, or even alarming they may become, should move one of the competitors to try to resolve it all by resorting to the immeasurably more costly and hazardous arbitrament of war is not easy to see, unless he happens to be greatly superior, in which case the competition should n not bother him. If the competition is downgraded to being only a potent contributing cause, then we should focus on what comes first and consider how much the arms competition really contributes. It may in fact derive from the prime cause, which we must assume to be political, in which case it is simply part of the working out of the animosity, that is, it is more an effect than a cause." (18)

Arms races lead to war because deterrence is governed by the probability equation, and is inherently unstable.

Here, he expresses disbelief that the cruise missile can cause a nuclear war:

"But the fate of ourselves and of the world is not going to hang on what we do or fail to do about some object like the cruise missile. Not long ago the alleged fate-determining object was the ABM. It sometimes helps to remember the several invasion panics in England in the mid-19th century, when the adoption of steam propulsion by war-ships was supposed to have created "a steam bridge across the Channel." (19)

The probability equations relating to unauthorized missile launches show that installing thousands of cruise missiles cannot help but increase the like-lihood of an unauthorized missile launch. Brodie inverts the error of induction. He assumes that what has not happened in the past won't happen in the future. He has forgotten his own argument that thermonuclear weapons have revolutionized war-fare.

Because Brodie just isn't aware of probability analysis, he continues to express doubts that arms races are dangers in themselves:

"If arms competitions are not in themselves dangerous, which is to say significantly provocative of an inclination to war, they are certainly costly." (20)

Brodie's thought is an excellent example of the thesis of this study. He looks at armamentspurely in terms of conventional deterrence analysis, and has no awareness of mathematical probability considerations.

Fortunately, Brodie's sense of history, and respect for the scientific me-thod, seem to prevent him from being dogmatic about his ideas. Toward the very end of his book he writes:

"The Unpredictability of the Outcome - "Consider the vast influence of accident in war, " Thucydides reports the Athenian ambassadors as saying, "before you are engaged in it...It is a common mistake in going to war to begin at the wrong end, to act first, and wait for disaster to discuss the matter." These words, written more than 2,300 years ago, might have saved much grief in the world if taken to heart by those who were tempted to believe otherwise. In wars throughout history, events have generally proved the pre-hostilities calculations of both sides sides, victor as well as loser, to have been seriously wrong. "Wars" as a modern writer puts it, "are the graveyards of the predictions concern-ing them."
Each generation of military planners is certain that it will not make the same kinds of mistakes as its forebears, not least because it feels it has profited from their example. Our own generation is convinced it

has an additional and quite special reason for being sure of itself: it is more scientific than its predecessors. Today the American armed forces are eagerly exploiting science and scientific techniques not only to avail themselves of new military tools of increasingly bizarre characteristics, the enthusiasm for which is itself a departure from former ways, but also to predict and analyze the tactics and strategy of future wars. It seems also to be a fact that in this repect the armed forces of the United States are considerably in advance of those of other nations, including our enemies. If so, it is an advantage of very large proportions.

The universe of data out of which reasonable military decisions have to be made is a vast, chaotic mass of technological, economic, and political facts and predictions. To bring order out of the chaos demands the use of scientific method in systematically exploring and comparing alternative courses of action. When the method is true to its own scientific tenets, it is bound to be more reliable by far than the traditional alternative method, which is to solicit a consensus of essentially intuitive judgements among experienced commanders." (21)

This attitude toward the scientific method is encouraging, and suggests that deterrence strategists may be willing ro recognize that the entire strategy of nuclear deterrence can be shown by scientific analysis to be unviable.

Herman Kahn

Herman Kahn's two books, On Thermonuclear War (1960), and On Escalation (1965) (22) are a strange mixture of insights regarding deterrence. Kahn has a talent for following-out ideas to their logical conclusions, which makes many of his thoughts and proposals seem outrageous to less imaginative and consistent readers. Also, he has a detached sense of humor, that in discussions of the excruciating tensions that can be created by nuclear arsenals, and the horrifying effects of nuclear war, often can be interpreted as callous. Probably because he has a background as a mathematician and physicist, Kahn uses mathematics more than any other deterrence strategist to make his points. He defends this practice in the preface to On Thermonuclear War:

"Some people appear to be very suspicious of calculations - and correctly so. I have written extensively elsewhere...on how quantitative analysis can lead either wittingly or unwittingly to error, but that does not mean that nonquantitative analyses are any less misleading. There is another reason for using numbers. The only way in which we can communicate even intuitive notions with any accuracy is to use quantitative measures." (23)

The central theme to both books probably follows from his consistency. Kahn realizes that if deterrence is to be more than a bluff, a nation that adopts it must be prepared to fight a nuclear war. He analyzes in great detail the conditions that might lead to such a war, the ways in which the war could be fought, and what levels of destruction the war might effect.

On the other hand, as we shall see, the books have a strong minor theme of pessimism about the ability of a protracted nuclear arms race to preserve peace.

Kahn realizes that deterrence always implies some probability of war (In our terms, that $p > 0$). In discussing the credibility of threats, he writes:

"It should be realized that a very low additional probability of war might not deter the Soviets. It is not as if there were no probability at all of war and their action had created this probability. It would be much more reasonable to say that just the existence of the U.S.-S.U. rivalry means that somehow there is always a probability of war or, say, one in fifty every year, and that if the Soviet action increased this by, in any one year, 50 per cent - from the assumed .02 to .03 - that this might not be, for many reasons, as deterring as raising the probability from zero to .01. As the engineer would put it, the increased probability of war must dominate "the noise level" to be deterring." (24)

But, he doesn't fully realize the most important consequence of this insight, that deterrence makes war probable. His lack of clear understanding of probability theory is strongly illustrated by the calculations that appear on page 40 of On Thermonuclear War:

How Much Tragedy is "Acceptable"?

BEFORE describing postwar problems, let us consider what we mean by an acceptable level of risk. We could start by asking, "How much tragedy can we live with and still not have 'the survivors envy the dead'?", but we will start with a more moderate question: "How dangerous or hostile a world would we be willing to live in and still call it a reasonable facsimile of a Russian or American standard of living?"

Nobody in either country would worry about a situation in which one thousand workers were engaged in some hazardous occupation which inflicted on each worker one chance in a hundred thousand per year of a fatal accident. Over a full year there would be approximately 99 chances in 100 that none of the workers would be hurt (see Table 5). Over a fifty-year period there would be better than an even chance that no worker would have been hurt. However, this attitude may change if the entire world population is subjected, as a result of some governmental action, to the same level of risk.

◆◆

TABLE 5
ACCEPTABILITY OF RISKS

Peace

$$1 \text{ thousand workers} \times \frac{1}{100,000} = 0.01/\text{year}$$

$$0.01 \times 50 \text{ years} = 0.5 \text{ workers}$$

$$3 \text{ billion people} \times \frac{1}{100,000} = 30,000/\text{year}$$

$$30,000 \times 50 \text{ years} = 1,500,000 \text{ people}$$

Postwar

$$180 \text{ million Americans} \times \frac{1}{100,000} = 1,800/\text{year}$$

$$1,800 \times 50 \text{ years} = 90,000 \text{ Americans}$$

◆◆◆

Because the world's population is so large (about three billion), one chance in a hundred thousand of a fatal accident per year means that on the average, 30,000 extra people per year would be killed. Over fifty years, 1,500,000 would die prematurely. While these are large numbers, something like this *might* result if many governments engaged in vigorous programs of weapons testing. Many people feel that any peacetime government action that could result in such a large number of casualties is intolerable.

(25)

Notice that Kahn assumes that if the chance of a fatal accident is one chance in a hundred thousand per hear, then in 50 years the probability of the accident calculates this way: $P = n \cdot p = 50 \times \frac{1}{100,000} = .0005$.

He's mistaken. The accident probability isn't a simple product of multiplying the probability for one year by the number of years, it's the more complex relationship given by the equation $P = 1 - (1-p)^n$. In this case:

$$P = .00001$$
$$n = 50$$

$$P = 1 - (1 - .00001)^{50} = 1 - (.99999)^{50} = .0004999$$

While it's true that the difference in the results produced by the two methods for calculating P isn't great, what's important is that Kahn gives no indication that he knows that his assumptions about how probability is calculated are in error. He did what seemed "natural," and the results gave him no clue about the error.

Kahn's partial understanding of mathematical probability theory may be the reason why he frequently expresses fear of accidental war:

"The accidental war is the one war in which both sides are most likely to get destroyed, partly because the war plans are likely to be inappropriate." (26)

And:

"...both for normal considerations of public safety and because of the possible catastrophic effects on our Type I Deterrence, it is crucially important that the operation of the force contain safeguards against the occurrence of an unauthorized explosion, safeguards which reduce the probability of this event to as close to zero as is humanly possible. This must be done even though it results in serious compromises and inefficiencies in the operation of the force. I use the words "unauthorized behavior" rather than "accident" because we must guard against many types of events - psychopathic or irrational individuals, mechanical or human failure, sabotage, irresponsible behavior, and so on. Some proposals (for example, unmanned space bombardment platforms or decentralized decision making on the issue of war or peace) do not take sufficient account of the necessity to prevent unauthorized behavior of either men or equipment." (27)

Kahn's uncertainty about probability theory is again suggested by the following passages about how the number of weapons, among other factors, affects accident proneness:

"Accident proneness may increase somewhat simply as a by-product of the number of alert weapons. However, the really dangerous intensification is likely to come from the proliferation of independent capabilities, each with its own standards of training, reliability of personnel, and safety practices." (28)

The equation, $P = 1 - (1-p)^{nm}$, tells us that increasing the number of weapons always will, not may, increase the chance of an accident.

Kahn's concern about the dangers of accidental war are expressed also in his analysis of the origin of World War I. He believes, as do many other historians, that the War is best understood as the culmination of a process of military preparedness that got out of hand. Europe's major powers had designed their war plans around railway timetables, and when one nation began to mobilize, a chain reaction led others to mobilize, and then to war. Whether or not one views this as the cause of World War I, or believes instead that the War was a deliberate act of aggression by Germany, there seems little doubt that all involved believed in "deterrence." Kahn quotes the British historian A.J.P. Taylor, writing in an Observer article:

"The statesmen of Europe with one accord accepted the theory of "the deterrent": the more strongly and firmly they threatened, the more likely they were both to preserve the peace of Europe and get their way...
...the German rulers were firmly wedded to the theory of the deterrent. A resolve to go to war, loudly proclaimed; and the other side would give way. In Jagow's words: "The more boldness Austria displays, the more strongly we support her, the more likely Russia is to keep quiet." (29)

Kahn's uneasiness with deterrence also is suggested by this discussion of nuclear proliferation, which uses the example of a ball balanced on a cup to illustrate the problem of stability:

"The widespread possession of nuclear weapons and delivery systems strikes many observers as similar to a situation that the physicist would describe as "semistable equilibrium." For example, imagine a ball balanced on top of a small cup so that small movements of the ball can be tolerated but not large ones. If this ball and the cup are isolated, it might sit there on top of its cup forever, but if it is submitted to the vagaries and chances of a sufficiently uncontrolled environment one can guarantee that sooner or later it will fall. This can be true even though every "reasonable" analysis of the situation that looks at probable or plausible disturbances showed that the forces were in close enough balance so the ball should stay were it is. It takes an improbable or implausible force to topple the ball. But some improbable and implausible events will occur and, barring a secular change in the situation, almost with certainty the ball will eventually fall." (30)

A few pages later, he expresses concern about an "uncontrolled arms race":

"...It should be clear to the reader at this point that the existence of an uncontrolled arms race, particularly one joined in by many nations, represents a very serious danger to both the U.S. and the S.U." (31)

In the same vein, after discussing the weapons systems that probably will have been built by the mid-'70s, he writes:

"...there are few who would believe that the kind of world just described could be stable for very long." (32)

and:

"I have been discussing the instability of deterrence in the face of a deliberate act on the part of the aggressor. On top of this must be added, unfortunately, instability due to the possibility of accident, miscalculation, sabotage, agents provocateurs, or the acts of mentally unbalanced individuals, or other kinds of unpremeditated war such as the catalytic, escalation and reciprocal fear of surprise attack. I think very few in 1950 would have been willing to predict that we would come to live in a world with 50,000 or even 5,000 buttons and never have a few of them pushed. Today, some believe it is possible, partly because experience has shown that such a situation is safer than we would have predicted, but mostly because they have to believe it or be very unhappy about the immediate future." (33)

Toward the end of On Thermonuclear War, Kahn becomes even more pessimistic about deterrence's ultimate ability to generate peace. It's specially suggestive that the following passage probably was written before 1960:

"...It is most unlikely that the world can live with an uncontrolled arms race lasting for several decades. It is not that we could not match Soviet expenditures; it is simply that as technology advances and as weapons become more powerful and more diverse, it is more likely that there will have to be at least implicit agreements on their use, distribution, and character if we are not to run unacceptably high risks of unauthorized or irresponsible behavior. No matter how antagonistic the Soviets feel toward us, they have common interests with us in this field. This does not mean that they will not try to exploit the common danger to obtain unilateral advantages;it simply means that there is an important area for bargaining here, one that we must fully exploit." (34)

Despite the doubts about deterrence's ultimate stability that Kahn expressed in On Thermonuclear War, five years later he published On Escalation. On Escalation is a systematic, theoretical discussion of threat-making, risk-taking, and war. Kahn sees 44 levels of conflict - an "escalation ladder" - along which nations in conflict can "progress", from "Ostensible Crisis" (Rung 1); "Political, Economic and Diplomatic Gestures: (Rung 2); and "Solemn and Formal Declarations" (Rung 3), to "Counter-value Salvo" (Rung 40), "Civilian Devastation Attack" (Rung 42), and "Spasm or Insensate War" (Rung 44). Like Tom Schelling, he believes that deterrence depends on making threats and taking risks. In On Escalation, Kahn is more optimistic about deterrence's ability to keep the peace than he was in On Thermonuclear War, perhaps because five more years without the explosion of a nuclear weapon in anger had led him to believe that "deterrence will work because it has worked."

In several passages, Kahn comes very close to expressing an understanding of the inherent instability of deterrence. Here, he shows again that he realizes that deterrence means that there's always a probability of war, and that this probability has some quantitative value within a given interval, in this case a week:

"In its most extreme form, the manipulation of the fear of inadvertent eruption might go as follows: Let us assume that two nations have such strategic systems and war plans that all-out war between them would be mutual homicide. Let us imagine that these two systems are built so that in a tense situation there is some probability, say one chance in a thousand per week, that they will go off accidentally. Assume also that both nations insist on maintaining this probability of total and mutual homicide until the other side backs down or compromises. We now have a situation in which there is an intense "competition in risk-taking."

An actual crisis situation would not be this stark. Nobody really knows what the probability of war is under different circumstances. We do not even know whether it goes up or down in a tense situation. It is, for example, quite conceivable that the extra care and concern associated with a tense situation might more than make up for the seeming extra danger that arises from weapons being on alert, from men operating under strain, and from the weakening which takes place in that important safeguard against accident, that high degree of"nuclear incredulity" which influences operators and decision-makers to disbelieve orders or signals that a nuclear war is under way. In practice, this strategy depends on an apparent increase in the probability or the risk of war, whether or not this actually occurs: it gives the impression that it is dangerous to allow the situation to drag out. In some cases, this apparent probability may in fact be a good objective estimate of the actual situation. In other cases, large and frightening as the apparent probability might be, it might be a serious underestimate of the actual risk of war. And in still other cases, it might be an overestimate of it.

While this concept of manipulating the risk of war in order to obtain foreign-policy advantages seems bizarre, the bizarreness comes from the scale of the threat and from its being made explicit. The tactic itself is used regularly, as the name of the threshold, "Don't rock the boat," suggests. Short of absolute surrender, or unilateral disarmament, there is always some probability, no matter how small, of inadvertent eruption, and whatever a nation does must affect this probability. It is also clear that affairs cannot be conducted in such a way as invariably to minimize this probability. Indeed, it sometimes is impossible to know for certain what actions would, in fact, minimize such a probability.

Fear of inadvertent war can be a very effective pressure partly because everybody knows that neither side really understands its present weapons systems or really appreciates the various ways in which an inadvertent war could occur. A rigorously realistic estimate of the risks that are run daily is impossible." (35)

As we've seen in Section I, a "rigorously realistic estimate of the risks that are run daily" isn't impossible.

Another example is this passage:

"The last objection to the upper rungs of the ladder of escalation concerns the long-term instability of such a system of international relationships. It is argued that if nations try to settle their disputes by climbing the escalation ladder, they eventually will find that they have climbed once too often, and an eruption will occur. This seems to me less an objection to the model than a valid objection to a process that is part of the real world." (36)

Contrary to what Kahn perceives, the deepest strategic objection to deterrence is to its theoretical model, to the notion that security can be maintained by a repetition of threats and risks, not to "a process that is part of the real world." The "real world" test of deterrence would seem to validate it as a strategy, "It will work because it has worked for more than 30 years." If a person wasn't aware of the actual operation of probability relationships, as shown by the mathematical model, $P = 1-(1-p)^n$, he or she might believe that

deterrence could provide security forever.

Kahn's discussion of the game of " chicken" also treats with the topic of repeated risk-taking. The game involves two drivers, each in a car, speeding toward each other. The driver who swerves to avoid a collision loses the game. Kahn believes that nuclear escalation differs from "chicken":

"In international relations, escalation is used to facilitate negotiations or to put pressure on one side or both to settle a dispute without war. If either side wanted a war, it would simply go to war and not bother to negotiate. For this reason, the common observation that "neither side wants war" is not particularly startling, even though it is often delivered with an air of revealed truth. Neither side is willing to back down, precisely because it believes or hopes it can achieve its objectives without war. It may be willing to run some risk of war to achieve its objective, but it feels that the other side will back down or compromise before the risk becomes very large.

"Chicken" would be a better analogy to escalation if it were played with two cars starting an unknown distance apart, traveling toward each other at unknown speeds, and on roads with several forks so that the opposing sides are not certain that they are even on the same road. Both drivers should be giving and receiving threats and promises while they approach each other, and tearful mothers and stern fathers should be lining the sides of the roads urging, respectively, caution and manliness.

There is another way in which escalation differs from these analogies. In escalation situations, both sides understand that they are likely to play repeatedly. Therefore (as discussed below), "systems bargaining" is important. Neither side wishes to gain an advantage at the cost of creating a psychological or political situation that will make eruption probable on the next play. Indeed, both sides may become anxious to work out some acceptable methods of adjudicating the game or to adopt general rules embodying some principles of equity or fairness. In fact, both sides may become so interested in getting such rules of procedure or rules of adjudication accepted that either side might be willing to lose a particular issue occasionally simply because trying to win that issue would set a precedent that would reduce the applicability of the basic rules.

In any case, the balance of terror is likely to work well enough to induce some degree of restraint and prudent behavior on each side. Precisely because both sides recognize that deterrence strategies are unstable, they are likely to refrain from testing the stability of the situation too often or too intensely, and to avoid the kind of behavior that might provoke an imprudent response from the other side. Both sides will understand that a strategy of deterrence requires the support of precedents and depends on widely understood and observed thresholds if it is to be reliable for any length of time." (37)

The passage contains contradictions and vaguaries. If the players recognize that deterrence strategies are unstable, why would they be playing them at all? What is the "length of time" during which the unstable balance of terror can be expected to be "reliable"?

Most of the book could be cited as an illustration of Kahn's lack of clear understanding of probability theory. Presumably, it is rational calculation, in, as Kahn calls it, "the Byzantine attitude of professionalism without heroics" (38), that enables nations to restrain themselves at different rungs of the escalation ladder. It seems more likely that the confusion and terror created by hundreds of nuclear explosions, and the radioactive "fog of war," would elevate the risks and chances of missile launches so rapidly that the progress upward along the ladder from rung to rung would be a spasmodic surge.

Glenn H. Snyder

The title, Deterrence and Defense, of Glenn H. Snyder's book (39) proclaims one of its main contributions to the literature of nuclear strategy. Snyder attempts to distinguish two main strategic problems that other strategists have tended to combine and confuse: deterrence and defense. "Deterrence" he defines as, "...discouraging the enemy from taking military action by posing for him a prospect of cost and risk outweighing his prospective gain." (40) "Defense" means, "...reducing our own prospective costs and risks in the event that deterrence fails." (41) Snyder then goes on to describe differences in strategy and weapons systems that are peculiar to problems of deterrence and defense, and how these interrelate.

Another contribution Snyder makes is to analyze the cost-gain "calculus" of both sides in a deterrence situation by means of mathematical models. These models involve positive or negative "payoffs." They don't take into consideration the fundamental probability considerations expressed in the equation, $P = 1 - (1-p)^n$.

Footnote 11, page 16, which refers to the models, makes abundantly clear that Snyder is unaware of the insights that mathematical probability analysis can provide in relation to deterrence:

"The numerical illustrations are intended simply to set out as starkly as possible the essential logic of deterrence; there is no intent to light a torch for the "quantifiability" of the factors involved, which are, of course, highly intangible, unpredictable, unmeasurable, and incommensurable except in an intuitive way. It is worth keeping in mind, however, that decision-makers do have to predict, to measure, and, in some sense, to make incommensurable factors commensurate if they are to reach wise decisions. Although, in practice, the factors cannot be given precise numbers, it is legitimate, for theretical purposes, to pretend that they can be in order to clarify the logic or method by which they should be weighed and compared. The logic is just as applicable to imprecise quantities as to precise ones; to express it in mathematical terms can provide a useful check on intuitive judgment and may bring to light factors and relationships which judgment would miss."

In the very first sentence of his section on "The Logic of Deterrence," Snyder assumes that deterrence situations involve a "probability of enemy military attacks":

"The object of military deterrence is to reduce the probability of enemy military attacks, by posing for the enemy a sufficiently likely prospect that he will suffer a net loss as a result of the attack, or at least a higher net loss or lower net gain than would follow from his not attacking." (42)

As we know, once he has done this, the factor p in the probability equation for authorized missile launches is greater than zero, and war will become probable within the strategic system being considered.

Snyder is unaware of the probability implications of his assumptions, in regard to both authorized and unauthorized missile launches. Later, he makes the familiar claim that a missile race can become more "stable" as the number of missiles increases. He doesn't acknowledge that increasing the number of missiles will always increase the likelihood of an unauthorized launch, or that large numbers of missiles will increase the destruction when war comes:

"...Thus, when the number of missiles on both sides is reasonably large, the requirement for a sufficient first-strike capability will be some multiple of the requirement for a minimum strike-back capability, and the multiple itself will be greater, the larger the number of the defender's missile sites...It is thus characteristic of the missile arms race, in seeming contrast to traditional arms races with conventional weapons, that it becomes more stable as it proceeds. The incentives to continue the arms race diminish rapidly as the numbers of weapons increase on both sides. The country which wishes to have only a minimum deterrent need have one that amounts to only a fraction of the opponent's striking force when the former's number of dispersed weapons is large relative to the number of weapons which could cause unacceptable damage to the opponent's cities...By similar reasoning, the country which contemplates a first strike can provide itself with the necessary capability only by resource expenditures very much larger than the expenditures the opponent must make to counter and re-establish the deterrent balance." (43)

Thomas C. Schelling

Thomas Schelling's book, Arms and Influence (1966) (44), emphasizes that deterrence is psychological, and relies on "the power to hurt." Many passages and even sections in the book show that Schelling is entirely unaware of mathematical probability analysis. A startling example is Chapter 3, "The Manipulation of Risk." In passage after passage, it's evident that Schelling doesn't understand what will tend to be the consequences of repeatedly threatening - taking risks with - nuclear war. He begins the chapter by describing an ideal situation that he believes would make nuclear war impossible, but actually would make its outbreak approach certainty:

"If all threats were fully believable (except for the ones that were completely unbelievable) we might live in a strange world - perhaps a safe one, with many of the marks of a world based on enforceable law. Countries would hasten to set up their threats; and if the violence that would accompany infraction were confidently expected, and sufficiently dreadful to outweigh the fruits of transgression, the world might get frozen into a set of laws enforced by what we could figuratively call the Wrath of God. If we could threaten world inundation for any encroachment on the Berlin corridor, and everyone believed it and understood precisely what crime would bring about the deluge, it might not matter whether the whole thing were arranged by human or supernatural powers. If there were no uncertainty about what would and would not set off the violence, and if everyone could avoid accidentally overstepping the bounds, and if we and the Soviets (and everybody else) could avoid making simultaneous and incompatible threats, every nation would have to live within the rules set up by its adversary. And if all the threats depended on some kind of physical positioning of territorial claims, trip-wires, troop barriers, automatic alarm systems, and other such arrangements, and all were completely infallible and fully credible, we might have something like an old fashioned western land rush, at the end of which - as long as nobody tripped on his neighbor's electric fence and set the whole thing off - the world would be carved up into a tightly bound status quo. The world would be full of literal and figurative frontiers and thresholds that nobody in his right mind would cross." (45)

In this often quoted passage, Schelling states that the effectiveness of deterrence depends on taking risks:

"There is just no foreseeable route by which the United States and the Soviet Union could become engaged in a major nuclear war. This does not mean that a major nuclear war cannot occur. It only means that if it occurs it will result from a process that is not entirely foreseen, from reactions that are not fully predictable, from decisions that are not fully under control...it is hard to see how a major war could get started except in the presence of uncertainty...
This is why deterrent threats are often so credible. They do not need to depend on a willingness to commit anything like suicide in the face of a challenge. A response that carries some risk of war can be plausible, even reasonable, at a time when a final, ultimate decision to have a general war would be implausible or unreasonable. A country can threaten to stumble into a war even if it cannot credibly threaten to invite one." (46)

Here, he describes a "real" situation in which the probability of war also approaches certainty. Schelling doesn't understand that continuous "competition in risk taking" means that war becomes probable:

"...there is a genuine risk of major war not from "accidents" in the military machine but through a diplomatic process of commitment that is itself unpredictable. The unpredictability is not due solely to what a destroyer commander might do at midnight when he comes across a Soviet (or American) freighter at sea, but to the psychological process by which particular things become identified with courage or appeasement or how particular things get included in or left out of a diplomatic package. Whether the removal of their missiles from Cuba while leaving behind 15,000 troops is a "defeat" for the Soviets or a "defeat" for the United States depends more on how it is construed than on the military significance of the troops, and the construction placed on the outcome is not easily foreseeable.

The resulting international relations often have the character of a competition is risk taking, characterized not so much by tests of force as by tests of nerve. Particularly in the relations between major adversaries - between East and West - issues are decided not by who _can_ bring the most force to bear in a locality, or on a particular issue, but by who is eventually _willing_ to bring more force to bear or able to make it appear that more is forthcoming." (47)

Schelling continues, comparing deterrence to Russian roulette. He's right that it's like Russian roulette, but what he doesn't realize is that the tendency for deterrence to end in nuclear war follows the same kind of probability curve as the tendency for Russian roulette to end in the death of one of the players:

"There are few clear choices - since the close of World War II there have been but a few clear choices - between war and peace. The actual decisions to engage in war - whether the Korean War that did occur or a war at Berlin or Quemoy or Lebanon that did not - were decisions to engage in a war of uncertain size, uncertain as to adversary, as to the weapons involved, even as to the issues that might be brought into it and the possible outcomes that might result. They were decisions to embark on a risky engagement, one that could develop a momentum of its own and get out of hand. Whether it is better to be red than dead is hardly worth arguing about; it is not a choice that has arisen for us or has seemed about to rise in the nuclear era. The questions that do arise involve _degrees of risk_ - what risk is worth taking, and how to evaluate the risk involved in a course of action. The perils that countries face are not as straightforward as suicide, but more like Russian roulette. The fact of uncertainty - the sheer unpredictability of dangerous events - not only blurs things, it changes their character. It adds an entire dimension to military relations; the manipulation of risk." (48)

Schelling's comments about the Cuban missile crisis display the same misunderstanding:

35

"...The Cuban crisis was a contest in risk taking, involving steps that would have made no sense if they led predictably and ineluctably to a major war, yet would also have made no sense if they were completely without danger. Neither side needed to believe the other side would deliberately and knowingly take the step that would raise the possibility to a certainty.

What deters such crises and makes them infrequent is that they are genuinely dangerous. Whatever happens to the danger of deliberate premeditated war in such a crisis, the danger of inadvertent war appears to go up. This is why they are called "crises." The essence of the crisis is its unpredictability. The "crisis" that is confidently believed to involve no danger of things getting out of hand is no crisis; no matter how energetic the activity, as long as things are believed safe there is no crisis. And a "crisis" that is known to entail disaster or large losses, or great changes of some sort that are completely forseeable [sic.] , is also no crisis; it is over as soon as it begins, there is no suspense. It is the essence of a crisis that the participants are not fully in control of events; they take steps and make decisions that raise or lower the danger, but in a realm of risk and uncertainty." (49)

Actually, a crisis is a situation in which risk is high, in which the value for p in the probability equation is large. Deterrence always makes p greater than zero. A crisis makes it greater than it usually is. That's why a nation is unlikely to survive many crises with nuclear deterrence. Schelling, unknowingly, puts his finger exactly on why deterrence is not a rational policy:

"...a contest in risk taking, involving steps that would have made no sense if they led predictably and ineluctably to a major war..."

In the following passage, Schelling indicates that he understands that war results from a process, but he apparently doesn't realize that the "process" is deterrence, a continuum of risk, in which p is neither zero nor 100%, but always has some value greater than zero:

"The idea, expressed by some writers, that such deterrence depends on a "credible first strike capability," and that a country cannot plausibly threaten to engage in a general war over anything but a mortal assault on itself unless it has an appreciable capacity to blunt the other side's attack, seems to depend on the clean-cut notion that war results - or is expected to result - only from a deliberate yes-no decision. But if war tends to result from a process, a dynamic process in which both sides get more and more deeply involved, more and more expectant, more and more concerned not to be a slow second in case the war starts, it is not a "credible first strike" that one threatens, but just plain war. The Soviet Union can indeed threaten us with war: they can even threaten us with a war that we eventually start, by threatening to get involved with us in a process that blows up into war." (50)

Schelling understands that "Brinksmanship" involves the manipulation of risk:

"If "brinksmanship" means anything, it means manipulating the shared risk of war. It means exploiting the danger that somebody may inadvertently go over the brink, dragging the other with him." (51)

However, he doesn't write that a continuous strategy of brinksmanship will quickly make war probable.

Further on, he begins a chapter section with the title "Nuclear Weapons and the Enhancement of Risk" (52). Enhancement of risk ultimately means increasing p's value. It means that war will become probable more rapidly.

Schelling expects the Soviet Union to compete in risk-taking, too:

"...we have to expect the Soviets to pursue their own policy of exploiting the risk of war. We cannot expect the Soviets to acquiesce in our unilateral nuclear demonstration. We have to be prepared to interpret and to respond to a Soviet nuclear "counterproposal." Finding a way to terminate will be as important as choosing how to initiate such an exchange. (We should not take wholly for granted that the initiation would be ours.)" (53)

And this passage is particularly noteworthy because it shows that Schelling doesn't realize that the principle of deterrence's inherent instability governs deterrence by conventional as well as by nuclear weapons. All of history that predated the invention of nuclear weapons can be seen as a series of wars that express the inherent instability of deterrence:

"...And it is the <u>character</u> of weapons as much as their quantity, probably more than their quantity, that makes the military environment stable or unstable. The character of military forces is partly determined by geography, partly by the way technology unfolds over time, partly by conscious choices in the design and deployment of military force.
     If all nations were self-sufficient islands with the pre-nuclear military technology of World War II, mutual deterrence could be quite stable; even a nation that had determined on war would not care to initiate it." (54)

In the same vein, consider the next quoted paragraph. It's certainly true that in a disarmed world people could re-create nuclear weapons in a time of crisis. But the re-creation of nuclear arsenals would simply bring back into existence nuclear deterrence and the nuclear arms race, which would serve no one's interest. If large numbers of people came to understand the mathematical probability laws that govern antagonistic nuclear arsenals, they likely will simply lose interest in all military solutions to international conflicts. Only a few decades ago, people believed in blood-letting as a cure for many diseases. Since medical science has shown that blood-letting decreases rather than increases the chance of recovering, the procedure has been abandoned. It's not that physicians don't know how to do it. They don't let blood because they know it won't achieve the desired results. Military force will be used as long as it's considered a route to security. When it's widely seen that it's a route to mutual annihilation, it will be discarded:

"Much of the interest in arms control among people concerned with military policy became focused in the early 1960s on the stability of mutual deterrence. Many writers on arms control were more concerned about the character of strategic weapons than the quantity, and where quantity was concerned their overriding interest was the effect of the number of weapons on the incentives to initiate war, rather than on the extent of destruction if war should ensue. A fairly sharp distinction came to be drawn between "arms control" and "disarmament." The former seeks to reshape military incentives and capabilities with a view to stabilizing mutual deterrence; the latter, it is alleged, eliminates military incentives and capabilities.

But the success of either depends on mutual deterrence and on the stability of that deterrence. Military stability is just as crucial in situations between unarmed countries as between armed ones. Short of universal brain surgery, nothing can erase the memory of weapons and how to build them. If "total disarmament" could make war unlikely, it would have to be by reducing incentives. It could not eliminate the potential. The most primitive war could be modernized by rearmament, once it got started." (55)

Schelling's lack of understanding of mathematical probability theory leads him into numerous errors. Perhaps the greatest is his belief that the calling of the nuclear strategist is to "manage risks." Risks certainly can be "managed," the value of p can be varied, but doing so isn't the route to permanently preventing nuclear war. No matter how intelligent, well informed, and thoughtful, the managers of the risks of deterrence are, nuclear war will become probable.

Samuel P. Huntington

In his article, "Arms Races: Prerequisites and Results" (56), Samuel P. Huntington distinguishes between quantitative and qualitative arms races. In quantitative arms races, states increase the number of existing arms. In qualitative arms races, the weapons are improved, or replaced by more effective weapons. Huntington believes that quantitative arms races are more likely to end in war than are qualitative ones. Also, he believes that war is more likely at the beginning of an arms race than later on:

"The danger of war is highest in the opening phases of an arms race, at which time the greatest elements of instability and uncertainty are present." (57)

He generalizes these conclusions this way:

"Assuming a fairly equal distribution of grievances, the likelihood of an arms race ending in war tends to vary inversely with the length of the arms race and directly with the extent to which it is quantitative rather than qualitative in character." (58)

Since he believes that armaments are an inherent characteristic of nation states, and, in the present situation, there are no international institutions for providing security in the place of individual national arms establishments, Huntington sees arms competition as inevitable. He believes that the greatest hope for peace lies in making the arms race between the United States and the Soviet Union qualitative rather than quantitative.

Huntington shows no awareness of the insights into arms races provided by

probability laws. The equation, $P = 1 - (1-p)^n$, shows that the longer an
arms race goes on, the more likely is the outbreak of war. It may be that the
greater number of uncertain factors at the onset of an arms race can make an attack by one side or the other more likely than during a similar interval later on,
but this probability can never be as great (unless it results in war) as that
which can be generated eventually by the exponential equation. This being the
case, the advantages of qualitative over quantitative competition eventually
are obliterated. New and more effective weapons are more destructive weapons.
This means that the qualitative arms race, although it may go on longer before
resulting in war, will result in a more destructive war than a quantitative arms
race. Late 19th and 20th century history offers an illustration. The exponential
development of science and technology have meant that 19th century arms races
tended to be quantitative, and those of the 20th century, qualitative. World
War I was more destructive than the Franco-Prussian War, and World War II was
more destructive than World War I, because of the increased power of weapons.
World War III, if it occurs, will be far more destructive than World War II,
although a greater period of time has elapsed since the end of World War II
than between 1918 and 1939.

Huntington's unawareness of probability theory seriously flaws his analysis.

Robert Jervis

In his article, "What Deters? The Ability to Inflict Assured Destruction"
(59), Robert Jervis notes that in a situation where both sides have nearly
equal nuclear forces, and hold each other's cities in hostage, the effectiveness of deterrence will depend more on variations in resolve and "will" than
on marginal increases in destructive hardware. Strengthening one's will means
being willing to take greater risks. He writes:

"The American deterrent is deterred by the fact that its cities are vulnerable, not by the fact that the Russians have some supposed military advantage. Since neither the United States nor the Soviet Union can take its
cities out of hostage, the state that is willing to run the greatest risks
will prevail. Many of those who call for the United States to match or sur-
pass the Soviets' nuclear arsenal are trying to have the United States com-
pensate for what they feel is a weakness of resolve by an excess in weaponry. But such a deficiency, if it exists, cannot be compensated." (60)

Jervis recommends "competition in risk taking" as the best way to make deterrence credible:

"Even if both sides recognize the greater determination of the side
defending the status quo, accidents and miscalculations are still possible, especially in situations growing out of a crisis in a third area.
To rely solely on assured destruction may be too dangerous. Some degree
of insurance can be purchased by a continuation of the present American
posture, which includes the availability of limited nuclear options. But
these should be demonstrations, keyed to competition in risk taking, not
attempts to wage a war of attrition; thus, the United States would not
have to match the Soviets on any of the standard measures of nuclear power. It does not take a superior or even an equal military force to show

by limited use that one is willing to take extreme measures rather than suffer a defeat. Such costs and risks are the trading chips of bargaining in the nuclear era; even if the United States had the weapons and doctrine for a flexible response policy, it could not avoid relying on them." (61)

Apparently, Jervis has neither intuition nor understanding of the realities that are the subject of mathematical probability analysis. He believes that the risk of catastrophe can be "intelligently" manipulated indefinitely without the catastrophe becoming probable. His mistake has appalling implications for civilization.

Patrick M. Morgan

Patrick M. Morgan's book, Deterrence (62), begins with a careful examination of the various definitions of deterrence. He starts with the simple notion that, "Deterrence involves manipulating someone's behavior by threatening him with harm." (63) After discussing various elaborations of this idea, he distinguishes between "pure deterrence" and "general deterrence":

"In the previous chapter a distinction was drawn between immediate or pure deterrence and general deterrence. The latter is the primary objective of military preparedness (when a state has no aggressive intent). The idea is to convince other states that, in principle, to use force against that state would not be congenial or rewarding. Of course a state also wishes to be militarily prepared to practice pure deterrence, but only when the outer barrier to attack posed by general deterrence has broken down. A pure deterrence situation emerges when a government realizes that another government is seriously considering an attack and mounts more specific threats of retaliation in an attempt to forestall it." (64)

Later, he discusses how bureaucratic processes, and the psychological characteristics of leaders may affect deterrence, and a variety of theories about what kind of deterrence is best. He comes down in favor of what he calls "sensible deterrence," expresses the view that it's unwise to trust peace to deterrence strategies, and concludes on a mild note of optimism:

"Revision of our thinking should proceed in the direction of reducing our own and the world's reliance on deterrence where we can, developing other types and patterns of international influence, and encouraging complexes of inter-dependence wherever possible coupled with reductions in nuclear and conventional forces. It is widely accepted that strategic nuclear arsenals have cancelled out their political/military utility, so that international political and military struggles proceed as if they were not even there. Many also believe that fears of escalation have made tactical nuclear weapons almost impossible to use as well. As a result, we may be in danger of complacently accepting the presence of such weapons. One key benefit of a sensible decision maker approach to deterrence is the recognition that government can be senseless, which could lead to a wider appreciation of the need for arms control to the point of substantial cutbacks in nuclear forces.

In this respect there are grounds for modest optimism. We may have turned the corner into an era in which, as Nixon liked to assert, a "generation of peace" is at hand. The implication is that the general deterrence relationships at the heart of the contemporary international system will be much more stable, not because deterrent threats are increasingly effective in the abstract but because the context has been altered. Key elements here would be a decline in great power challenges to the legitimacy of the international system, greater preoccupation with domestic matters for most system members, and increasing domestic stability for most political systems. Under such circumstances, there would be fewer occasions where immediate deterrence was put to the test, particularly as confrontations among great powers gave way to the atmosphere of detente.

If all this comes to pass and is self-sustaining, then it will mean we have - luckily, accidentally, improbably - passed through an era of extreme instability in domestic systems due to the aftermath of war, the collapse of empires, and the emergence of new states. And it was dominated by widespread challenges to the legitimacy and structure of the international system. To get through the recurrent crises and confrontations of this century, the world's governments increasingly relied on deterrence via weapons of steadily rising destructiveness, guided by a doctrine that fortified our confidence in deterrence just as the potential consequence of its collapse reached outlandish proportions. It was confidence badly misplaced.

Having gotten through this era , we should not permit continued reliance on deterrence on such a scale to continue. We should work toward dismantling a good part of nations' deterrence machinery while stressing other kinds of international relationships. If instead we permit reliance on deterrence to spread, in the end we can predict further periods of danger and instability when deterrence somewhere breaks down, periods in which some or all of civilization is immediately at risk." (65)

Like other deterrence strategists, Morgan regards deterrence mainly as a psychological phenomenon, in which rational decisions are made as the result of calculations of gains and losses. While he recognizes that deterrence can be a dangerous policy, he doesn't employ mathematical probability analysis to try and find out how dangerous.

Morgan's lack of awareness of probability theory is strikingly evident in his examination of definitions of deterrence. Here, he accepts the notion that governments that are thinking about an attack make the attack "possible":

"Deterrence then becomes an attempt to use threats of retaliation to induce "sensible" decision making in a severe crisis, to get an opponent to make a decision on whether or not to attack in a way that would pretty much rule out taking such a drastic and uncertain step. A signal defect in deterrence is that it is practiced on governments that have already given some thought to an attack, that is, some set of circumstances has had the effect of making it entirely possible that such a non-incremental step could be taken." (66)

He defines a "pure deterrence" situation as one that includes these four conditions. Note that condition (3) includes the idea of "distinct possibility," a notion that means that in the probability equation, $P = 1-(1-p)^n$, p70:

"(1) In a relationship between two hostile states the officials in at least one of them are seriously considering attacking the other or attacking some area of the world the other deems important.

(2) Key officials of the other state realize this.

(3) Realizing that an attack is a distinct possibility, the latter set of officials threaten the use of force in retaliation in an attempt to prevent the attack.

(4) Leaders of the state planning to attack decide to desist primarily because of the retaliatory threat(s)." (67)

Had Morgan understood the insights regarding deterrence theory that are provided by mathematical probability theory, he might have been less optimistic that the world has passed through the most dangerous phase regarding deterrence's "stability," and even more anxious to have the machinery of deterrence dismantled as quickly as possible.

Richard Rosecrance

Richard Rosecrance's article, "Strategic Deterrence Reconsidered" (1975) (68), is largely a review of the history and theory of deterrence. Rosecrance emphasizes a point made by Robert McNamara in 1968, that the ability to deter is a function of the relationship between "assured destruction capability" and credibility. Rosecrance argues that these factors must be kept at a minimum level. If one or the other decreases, the other must increase to maintain the level. Rosecrance points out that it's unlikely that the U.S. again will have overwhelming weapons superiority, and therefore the factor of credibility will tend to be emphasized. He cites Schelling's theory of risk manipulation as an approach to increasing credibility, and observes that such a policy places one on the "slippery slope to the abyss," and may involve "taking serious risks to protect less than fundamental values."

Rosecrance devotes considerable space to analyzing "bipolar" (two-country) deterrence, in distinction to "multi-polar" (many country) deterrence situations. He notes the dangers of accidental war, and concludes that if multipolar deterrence is to succeed, the powers that are friendly toward each other must augment their deterrence postures with strong political ties. He concludes that a multipolar world will become very violent if the major powers do not cooperate with one another.

Rosecrance's analysis is unusual because it points toward the conclusions of mathematical probability analysis without involving probability equations. Rosecrance senses that there's something wrong with a policy of trying to achieve security by manipulating risk, and sees that proliferation, increasing the number of independent nuclear arsenals, will increase the risks. His analysis doesn't leave him confident about deterrence's ultimate ability to prevent nuclear war.

Paul H. Nitze

In an April 13, 1982 <u>New York Times</u> article opposing a nuclear weapons freeze, Paul H. Nitze, long-time governmental deterrence strategist and arms control specialist, wrote:

"Deterrence has worked. To remove the essential prop of nuclear deterrence prior to rectification of the conditions that led to its fashioning would be to tempt fate." (69)

Nitze makes the philosophic error of believing that deterrence will work because it has worked. In regard to "tempting fate," a person who rolls dice, or plays Russian roulette, is a perfect example of someone who tempts fate. Nitze's lack of awareness of how mathematical probability theory relates to deterrence strategy leads him to support extremely dangerous policies, and oppose policies that might reduce the risk of catastrophic war.

Alexander M. Haig, Jr.

In a speech delivered April 6, 1982, at the International Club of Georgetown University's Center for Strategic and International Studies, then Secretary of State Alexander M. Haig, Jr. made a number of statements that showed that he was unaware of the implications to deterrence theory of mathematical probability analysis. Essentially, the speech is a defense of deterrence. The main reason Haig gives for believing in deterrence is that deterrence "works":

"Deterrence has been supported because deterrence works. Nuclear deterrence and collective defense have preserved peace in Europe, the crucible of two global wars in this century. Clearly neither improvement in the nature of man nor strengthening of the international order have made war less frequent or less brutal. Millions have died since 1945 in over 130 international and civil wars. Yet nuclear deterrence has prevented a conflict between the two superpowers, a conflict which even without nuclear weapons would be the most destructive in mankind's history." (70)

and:

"The strategy of deterrence has kept the peace for over 30 years. It has provided the basis for arms control efforts. And it offers the best chance to control and reduce the dangers we face." (71)

Haig sees international relations management as taking a series of risks, sometimes very high risks, with nuclear bargaining chips:

"Let us also recall that nuclear deterrence must work not just in times of peace and moments of calm. Deterrence faces its true test at the time of maximum tension, even in the midst of actual conflict. In such extreme circumstances, when the stakes on the table may already be immense, when Soviet leaders may feel the very existence of their regime is theatened, who can say whether or not they would run massive risks if they believed that in the end the Soviet state would prevail." (72)

Apparently, Haig was prepared to repeatedly take "massive risks." The spirit of brinksmanship lives on.

Haig makes the philosophic error of induction in believing that a policy will work because it has worked. He makes a scientific error in believing that a stable policy for avoiding catastrophe can include repeatedly risking the catastrophe.

Colin S. Gray

Colin Gray is director of national security studies at the Hudson Institute, the research center founded by Herman Kahn. It's therefore natural to expect Gray's thinking and writing style to resemble Kahn's. Like Kahn, Gray believes that for deterrence to be more than a bluff, the U.S. must be prepared to fight a nuclear war. Therefore, he advocates civil defense, as well as the installation of accurate counterforce weapons such as the MX. He believes that U.S. strategic thinking is poor, in that it tends to accept a balance of terror and "mutually assured destruction" as the best of possible situations. Gray wants "victory." He wants to defeat the Soviet Union, to destroy totalitarian communism. He believes that this can be done without waging nuclear war by containing Soviet aggressive tendencies by means of military threats, and applying economic and military pressures to force Soviet society to "crack."

Gray believes completely in the ancient precept, "If you want peace, prepare for war." He's unconvinced that the arms race is a serious danger, "Even if this author is incorrect in believing that the arms race should not be reified as a danger to mankind..." (73), and "...the idea that there is a malevolent "arms race" that is the danger is almost entirely misleading." (74) Also, he believes that the arms race isn't inherently unstable:

"The most obvious deficiency in the arms race instability theory is the fact that nobody, inside or outside of government, has yet designed a convincing model of the dynamics of the Soviet-American arms competition." (75)

Gray can write this sentence because he has no understanding of mathematical probability theory. Like Thomas Schelling, he believes that threats and risk can be "managed" indefinitely without catastrophe occurring. Absent insights into why repeatedly taking risks makes war probable, Gray's worldview seems airtight. It enables him to observe jauntily that the MX will give "cardiac arrest to Soviet targeteers." (76) Once it's understood that deterrence is inherently unstable, that authorized and unauthorized missile launches become probable, that increasing the number of nuclear weapons increases the likelihood of at least an unauthorized missile launch, his position is revealed to be about the most dangerous possible to U.S. institutions and values.

While Gray is accumulating enormous arsenals of accurate missiles in the confidence that "victory" is just a matter of time, the reality is that time is steadily increasing the probability of catastrophic nuclear accidents and catastrophic war. Gray's position is a striking example of the possible dangers in an incomplete analysis, one that ignores mathematical probability theory.

V. Conclusions

"Wars occur out of chains of often highly improbable events..."

- Colin S. Gray ([1])

It's evident from this review of the writings of eminent deterrence strategists that none has been deeply aware of the mathematical probability principles that are the core of this analysis. All have made the mistake of believing that risk can be manipulated safely, that it's possible to repeatedly risk catastrophe without the catastrophe occurring. Indeed, the spiritual heart of deterrence can be described as the conviction that through intelligence, knowledge, discipline, sacrifice, and courage, the world can be kept safe forever by threatening and being prepared to conduct, nuclear war.

Why have strategists made this error? Possibly because their psychological speculations have seemed to produce convincing insights. Possibly because some of them have wanted to believe that deterrence will work, and this has distorted their perceptions. Possibly because it's not been obvious that deterrence is ruled by mathematical probability laws.

The equations model a deceptive situation. They show how the probability of an event proceeds from zero to near certainty. Until the event occurs, there's no evidence of it at all. Furthermore, if the probability of the event is looked at over a small interval, that probability may always appear low, or " safe." As we've seen, the daily probability of strategic deterrence failing can be no higher than about .006%. Without an understanding of the probability equations, who would believe that we would be in a dangerous situation if the daily chance of a given missile being launched is only one in one-hundred-million?

If the probability of an event always seems very low, it's natural to feel that the event won't occur. The curve below shows this:

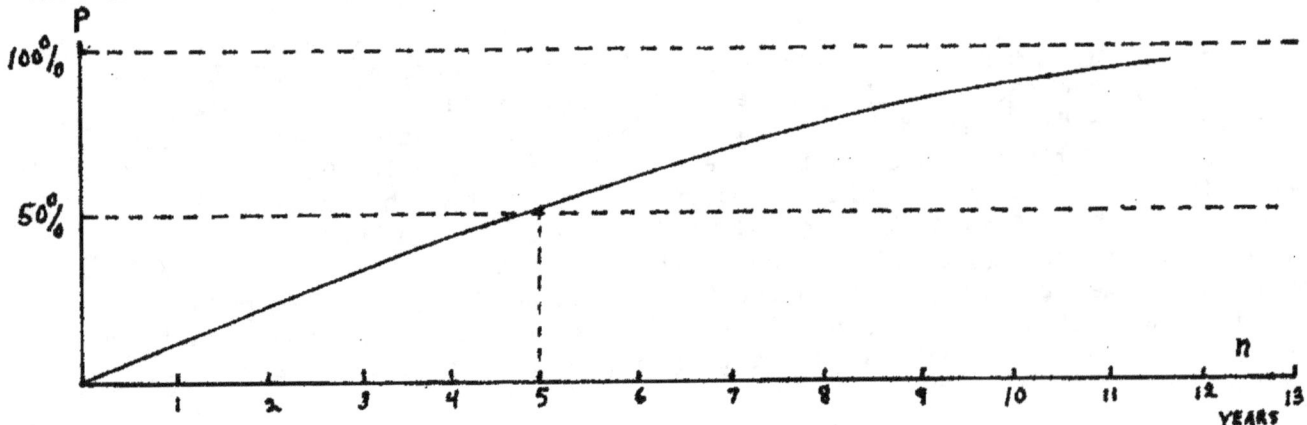

The event being modeled is improbable within a period of five years. In a period of ten years, it's highly probable.

Still another reason may be related to technological development within our civilization. As we've seen, calculations based on the probability equations can involve raising decimal fractions with large numbers of digits to very high powers. This is difficult to do without the aid of an electronic calculator (2). Early calculators were huge computers, so expensive that few people could own them. These computers were used only for projects that were judged to have a high priority for business or the military. It's only in the last ten years that it's been possible for nearly everyone to purchase pocket calculators with the needed calculating power. It may be that the task of deriving quantified results from the equations has looked so formidable that people haven't undertaken it. I know that my interest in the equations was stimulated greatly by being able to make some assumptions concerning n's and p's values, punch them into a calculator, and have a result within a second or two.

Whatever the reason or reasons may be, nuclear arsenals that have the capacity to quickly destroy civilization have been created, and their use approaches certainty. What is the rational response to this situation?

A variety of responses are possible. One is to continue deterrence and the arms race in the hope that the "enemy" will collapse before nuclear war breaks out. The "free world" version of this strategy, that can be represented by the thought of Colin Gray and Richard Pipes (3), is that the rigid, totalitarian political system, and inefficient socialist economy of the Soviet Union will be unable to sustain the drains and pressures of a prolonged, high-technology arms race. Eventually, class tensions, and the grievances of only partially absorbed ethnic and nationality groups, will lead to revolution and the overthrow of communism.

The communist version is that capitalist societies inevitably will develop severe internal class conflicts, undergo revolutions, and evolve into socialist societies.

These models are ~~remarkably~~ similar. Both resort to historical analysis, include a great deal of speculation, and are invigorated by large doses of hope. Neither has a foundation in mathematical probability analysis.

Continuing deterrence in the hope that either of these models will "pan out" involves risking the extinction of the human species. The rational nature of such an activity is dubious. Some people might feel that it's better to terminate the human experiment rather than risk world domination by communism or capitalism. It seems likely that most people would rather create a situation that would guarantee human existence and hence the possibility of a continuing struggle for political liberty and economic justice. Once everyone is dead, value preferences, moral arguments, and political activity are impossible as well as pointless.

A second strategy is to let deterrence run its course, and to try and survive nuclear war. Two strategies exist for surviving nuclear war. One is to build impregnable defenses against nuclear weapons. The other is to try and reduce the damage of the war as much as possible, "win" it, and rebuild the nation afterwards.

Building impregnable defenses against nuclear weapons is so difficult that most authorities believe it impossible (4). Any defense must be nearly 100% effective to prevent devastation. For example, the Soviet Union has approximately 2,000 strategic missiles. One percent of these could destroy the 20 largest cities in the United States, and radioactively contaminate vast areas. Such destruction would be a national catastrophe. Ten percent of the missiles, or 200 of them, could virtually obliterate the United States as a social unit. Yet, defenses that permitted only ten percent of the missiles to get through still would be 90% effective. Such a high level of effectiveness is unheard of in the history of anti-aircraft defense(5), the only kind of widely field-tested defense that we have to compare with anti-missile defenses. In World War II, anti-aircraft defenses that destroyed ten percent of attacking forces were effective enough to make continued attacks prohibitively costly. That level of effectiveness was achieved in only a few places, although most World War II planes flew less than 300 mph, and nations had several years to field-test their anti-aircraft weapons. Anti-missile weapons would have to be nearly 100% effective without field testing against targets travelling 20,000 miles an hour, and capable of a variety of tactics for penetrating the defenses.

Penetration tactics could include launching swarms of missiles to "saturate" or "override" the defenses, giving missiles and warheads evasive maneuver capabilities, launching dummy missiles to fool the defenses, broadcasting radio-reflective materials such as tiny bits of tin foil to "blind" defense radar screens and guidance systems, and using the electromagnetic pulses from exploding nuclear weapons to destroy the solid-state circuitry of defense detection, guidance, and communications systems.

Laser and particle-beam defense systems, that have been heralded as potentially perfect missile-killers, have fundamental weaknesses (6). If they are land-based, cloudy, rainy, or snowy weather can disrupt them. If space-based, they can be destroyed by hunter-killer missiles and satellites, saturated, or frustrated by covering attacking missiles and warheads with rotating, reflective shields.

In sum, despite President Reagan's optimistic pronouncements, no sufficiently effective defenses against missiles exist, or are in prospect.

Even if effective anti-ballistic missile defenses could be built, an attacker still would have a nearly endless variety of methods for delivering warheads. Air-breathing, "cruise" missiles can carry large warheads, deliver them with pinpoint accuracy, and are inexpensive compared to ICBMs. An attack might consist of tens of thousands of cruise missiles launched at night or in bad weather.

Or, if all missile defenses were "airtight," an "enemy" still could fabricate monster bombs of hundreds of megatons power, and install them off the coasts of the United States. Such weapons would be inexpensive, and only a few of them, by generating great tidal waves, and radioactive clouds, could destroy all coastal areas.

Still another way of delivering weapons to their targets is to smuggle them into cities, and areas near military installations, before the war occurred. Thermonuclear bombs of great power can be made so small that several could be stored in a closet. Bombs also could be put in automobiles, vans, packing-cases, trunks, and even large suitcases.

Ever since the invention of nuclear weapons, the advantage has swung in favor of the offense and against defense. Bombs now can be made of any size, and delivered by many techniques. For every defense that's created, an off-setting attack can be devised, and the means of attack are less expensive than the means for defense. Devising defenses against nuclear weapons is a losing battle.

What would a strategy of mitigating the effects of nuclear war, "winning" the war, and rebuilding the nation afterwards, involve? Some 20 years ago, Herman Kahn discussed such a strategy in On Thermonuclear War. The strategy divided the nation into an A country that was destroyed by the war, and a B country that survived, and rebuilt the nation afterwards. An attack today could either completely destroy the B as well as the A country, or leave so little left that recovery would be impossible.

Even if highly effective missile defenses could be built, preparing to survive, "win", and recover after a nuclear war would require a major national effort, far greater than the efforts exerted to win the first and second world wars. It would be necessary to relocate or duplicate underground, key administrative, military, and industrial facilities, and large amounts of strategic materials. Beyond that, it would be necessary to sell the population on experiencing and trying to survive a nuclear war. It's highly unlikely that the people of the United States would accept such a strategy. They support deterrence because they believe it will work. If their government told them that deterrence was going to fail, and they should begin preparing to survive a nuclear war fought with thousands of missiles, it's unlikely that many would still support deterrence or the government.

Also, preparing for nuclear war would make war more probable. It would greatly weaken diplomatic efforts to prevent the war, and would frighten the "enemy" into a similar program. Preparation on both sides would tend to become "crash" programs. If war was seen as inevitable and imminent, preemptive strategies would dominate.

In addition, the strategy of "weathering" nuclear war has no long-run value. If the principle of deterrence remains, and nations continue to build nuclear weapons, the probability equations show that nuclear war I would be followed by nuclear wars II and III. The limited power of conventional weapons has permitted world civilization to survive cycles of wars, even world wars, in the past. Cycles of nuclear wars can't be survived. At some point, the radioactivity in the atmosphere and on the ground would reach levels lethal to all but the most primitive living things.

If trying to cope with nuclear war isn't realistic, what strategy is? A strategy for preventing nuclear war.

Arms control is such a strategy. Arms control strategies seek to prevent war by bringing the arms race "under control." Examples are the Salt I and Salt II treaties, and versions of the proposal to "freeze" deployment and development of nuclear weapons systems. None of these strategies takes into consideration the probability equations. Therefore, all represent misunderstandings of the situation. Their advocates regard an uncontrolled nuclear arms race as the great danger to peace. In the main, they accept deterrence and believe in "stable deterrence." They don't acknowledge that all deterrence strategies lead toward nuclear war and are inherently unstable.

Nevertheless, arms control is correct in recognizing that an uncontrolled arms race is a great danger in itself. It means more missiles, and more vulnerable retaliatory capabilities. Also, it means nuclear proliferation, putting nuclear weapons into the hands of governments that may be "irresponsible." All of these developments will hasten the outbreak of nuclear war. Even though arms control strategies don't fully recognize the limitations of deterrence, they would at least "buy time" if adopted.

The best arms control strategies would reduce arsenals the most and the quickest. This is because the probability of an unauthorized missile launch is decreased by decreasing the number of missiles, as the equation, $P = 1 - (1-p)^{nm}$, and graph

VI, page 11 show, and because small arsenals will cause less damage than large ones. Rapid reduction is necessary to reduce the effect of the time factor, n, in the equation.

Another difficulty with arms control strategies lies in their need for verification and inspection. There are two main kinds of inspection. "National technical means" can be carried out by means of satellites, airplanes, and seismographic equipment. They work best when there are large numbers of large nuclear weapons that can be readily detected. Arguments for the freeze are that silos of the current, large, land-based missiles can be easily photographed, and that there are so many missiles that small infractions or "cheating" won't significantly affect the weapons balance.

"Cooperative" inspection is " on-site," and can involve people inspecting weapons and weapons bases, to make sure that there are agreed-on numbers of weapons and warheads.

As nuclear arsenals are reduced, both kinds of inspection become more difficult. Also, as Henry Kissinger and other strategists have pointed out, small arsenals make small numbers of weapons decisive. Therefore, at some point in arms control, inspection simply won't guarantee equality and security.

The probability equations show that the only way to prevent nuclear war is to de-activate all nuclear weapons. If strategies of continuing the arms race, and arms control, can't de-activate nuclear weapons, we are left with disarmament strategies as the only possibilities.

Disarmament strategies are of two kinds, multilateral and unilateral. Multilateral strategies are similar to arms control, and rely on verification and inspection. In regard to nuclear arsenals, they break down when the presence or absence of nuclear weapons can't be ascertained. Because of this, the complete deactivation of nuclear arsenals is possible only through unilateral disarmament. Nations must decide to de-activate their nuclear arsenals regardless of agreements or verification arrangements.

Unilateral disarmament has two slightly different forms, "unilateral initiatives," and unilateral disarmament. Being aware of the differences between these strategies helps in understanding the literature about disarmament and arms control, particularly that written in the late '50s and early '60s.

Unilateral initiatives' is a technical term used to describe a unilateral disarmament program undertaken as a gesture to encourage trust between nations, and to set the stage for disarmament negotiations. In this context, an "initiative" doesn't jeopardize the military posture of the nation undertaking it, and is reversible. An example would be NATO or Warsaw Pact troop reductions. The problem with unilateral disarmament of this kind is that it can be regarded as a ruse, and therefore probably won't have much effect.

Usually, "unilateral disarmament" is meant to mean disarmament by one side that isn't reversible, and will weaken its military posture.

Unilateral nuclear disarmament immediately raises questions about the practicality of conventional forces. Since conventional forces are no match for an "enemy" armed with nuclear weapons, there would seem little point in retaining conventional forces. As Japan found out in 1945, waging war with conventional forces against a nuclear power invites a nuclear attack as well as certain defeat. In addition, conventional forces are expensive. In view of this, a nation that embarked on unilateral nuclear disarmament might as well continue disarming down to the police level.

Therefore, pursuing national security in the nuclear age has brought us to complete unilateral disarmament. This isn't strange, if it's remembered that nuclear armaments are the extentions of conventional ones, and nuclear deterrence is an extension of the deterrence strategies that have governed the development of conventional arsenals throughout history. Once it can be shown that nuclear deterrence will result in the destruction of civilization, and eventually the human species, conventional arsenals, and the principle of military force, are no longer rational.

It's this understanding that must lie at the foundation of any realistic and rational national security program. Military force is obsolete as a route to national security. In a highly sophisticated scientific and technological society, deterrence and military competition lead to the destruction of the nation, civilization, and the species.

If abolishing military strategies and institutions seems impossible and unwise, perhaps the knowledge of how to make nuclear weapons and missiles can be wiped out. The world then could return to conventional armies, conventional deterrence, and conventional wars. No one has suggested that this is possible. As Herman Kahn has pointed out, only lobotomizing the entire human race could eliminate the knowledge of how to manufacture nuclear weapons. Furthermore, the growth of scientific and technological knowledge is exponential. Ever more powerful weapons are on the horizon, and no end can be seen to weapons development. There is no way to avert nuclear war other than the abandonment of all forms of military force, and the creation of political, non-military institutions that can resolve conflicts without war.

There are three main theories for achieving justice and security without the use of military force: Democratic world government, sometimes called "liberal political theory"; Marxism/Leninism; and humanitarian anarchism. Liberal political theory sees war as the inevitable consequence of "international anarchy"; independent nation states pursuing their interests with private armies. Peace can be achieved only if the nations are willing to give part of their sovereignty, and all of their military force, to a single world authority. This world authority, or government, would have the power to make and enforce laws, and would seek the interest of all of its citizens - the world population. The idea that peace depends on government is found in the writings of Hobbes, Locke, Rousseau, and other 17th and 18th century political philosophers, and is at the heart of the political thinking that's created the western, constitutional democracies. Its outstanding success was the joining of the American colonies into the United States.

Marxism/Leninism sees all social conflict and injustice as the result of the class divisions generated by capitalism. It explains war as the consequence of imperialism, the struggle between capitalist states over resources and markets. According to Marxist/Leninist theory, once communism has replaced capitalism, classes will be abolished, competitive, wasteful economic practices will be supplanted by cooperative, efficient, social ones, and there'll be no occasion for wars. Although Marxist/Leninist theory sees a need for military force for revolutionary purposes, and to protect communist states against counter-revolutionary attacks by capitalist ones, it predicts that when communism's universal, there'll be no international conflict, and the need for armed forces will fade away. Along the same lines, Marxist/Leninist theory predicts that in a classless society, without conflict of economic and social interest, there'll be no need for the police and other internally coercive state institutions. In time, these, too, will "wither away."

In practice, communist nations have proven bellicose toward each other. Russia and China are enemies; China is more of an ally of the United States than a friend of the Soviet Union. China and Vietnam have fought one major war, and another seems imminent. Vietnam has overrun most of Cambodia.

All communist states have large police forces, and other powerful institutions for regimenting their people and repressing dissent. The decrease of police terrorism in the Soviet Union since Stalin's death, and the current Chinese regime's denouncement of the coercive policies of the "Cultural Revolution," and "Gang of Four," are examples of progress in these societies toward less severe coercion. There's little evidence that coercive state institutions will die out entirely in the communist countries.

Humanitarian anarchism has always been a significant strain in the Christian tradition. Protestant sects, such as the Mennonites, advocate it. Other examples are Tolstoi's religious writings, and the Catholic Worker movement founded by Dorothy Day and Peter Maurin. Thoreau's writings suggest it. Gandhi's nonviolent movement in India, which included the idea of a nation made up of hundreds of thousands of self-governing, self-sufficient villages, implied it. Humanitarian anarchism seeks to generate social justice and stability purely by nonphysically coercive means. These movements tend to be pacifist, not admitting the need for military force. Although it's worked in small communities, humanitarian anarchism has known no large-scale successes.

These different political theories are rooted partly in different appraisals of "human nature." Liberal political theory has a pessimistic view. It sees human nature as always including strong selfish, egotistical motivations (7). It regards selfishness as inherent, perhaps genetic. While it can be reduced by favorable social conditions, it can never be entirely eliminated. In the absence of government, people live competitively, like predatory beasts in the jungle. Government tames and channels the selfish, egotistical, violent impulses.

Marxism/Leninism sees human nature as malleable, entirely the product of conditioning, of culture. People brought up in capitalist societies will be competitive, individualistic, egotistical, and cruel. Those reared in socialist ones will be cooperative and caring.

Humanitarian anarchists see human nature as basically loving, generous, kindly and sociable. The selfish, egotistical, and cruel characteristics that are so commonplace they regard as corruptions wrought by coercive and exploitative institutions.

Nonviolent resistance is a political power theory developed in the humanitarian anarchist tradition. Etienne de la Boétie, Tolstoi, and Thoreau suggested it. Gandhi systematized and experimented widely with it. Nonviolence proposes to overcome or transform the selfish, violent and cruel characteristics of an "enemy's" attitude by means of "truth force," courageous, nonviolent confrontation.

People who are aware of these different outlooks usually regard the social goals of humanitarian anarchism as desirable ideals that for various reasons can't yet, or never can be, attained. This suggests that if we wish to progress from a world that's burdened with nuclear armaments, and threatened with catastrophic nuclear war, to one that's not threatened by war and has a chance to evolve, the evolution we want is in the direction of humanitarian anarchism.

If this evolution is to occur, it must be motivated by the analysis of military power and deterrence that we have undertaken, for without it, there will be no incentive for advocates of the liberal political theory and Marxist/Leninist viewpoints to change their policies.

Although disarmament can reduce the likelihood of cataclysmic nuclear war, it can't prevent military force from being used to blackmail, or to invade another country. Therefore, any society that adopts unilateral disarmament also would be wise to develop programs to decrease the likelihood of, and to resist, blackmail and invasion. The best program probably would include at least four elements:

1. Worldwide publication of the realities revealed by the probability equations. This would demonstrate the need to deactivate nuclear weapons, and pursue nonmilitary solutions to conflicts;

2. A call for democratic world government;

3. Large scale economic aid programs to end involuntary poverty;

4. Preparation for nonviolent resistance to cope with the possibility of invasion and occupation.

World government would offer at least an intirim political structure within which conflicts could be resolved justly without military force. Also, it would provide for the evolution of society in a non-coercive direction as far as social and biological realities would permit. Although different political perspectives are rooted to a large degree in different theories of "human nature," there's no way ultimately to test these theories. For example, is selfishness a cultural or genetic phenomenon? What test can tell? Culture can be attributed to genetic factors. Genetic factors can be attributed to natural selection within a given environment or culture. Since the problem's unsolvable, the most that can be done is to set up a structure that can evolve as far as possible in the direction of unselfishness. Democratic world government can do this. Once established, it would either stabilize itself at some balance between coercion and freedom, if selfishness had a genetic origin, or its coercive elements would "wither away," as the cultural causes of selfishness and violence were progressively removed. World government could achieve this while national governments have been unable to, because it would be free of the pressures generated by military institutions. In both democratic and communist societies, the coercion and cruelty implicit in military institutions has set a limit beyond which the society can't evolve in a non-coercive direction. In order to maintain their positions in arms races, and to sustain deterrence policies, all nations have had to profoundly compromise their humanitarian traditions.

In regard to the programs to eliminate poverty, all three perspectives tend to regard involuntary poverty as a major cause of violence and war. The economic aid programs would be administered through the United Nations to both insure that they wouldn't be used to promote narrow nationalist interest, and to strengthen the U.N. as a nucleus for world government.

Any nuclear superpower could couple such a four-point program with unilateral disarmament. If it did, what consequences could it expect? It probably wouldn't suffer a counterforce attack. There'd be no forces to destroy. In this regard, it helps to remember that the surprise attack on Pearl Harbor was a counterforce blow directed at the Seventh Fleet, and its supporting installations.

Also, the nation probably wouldn't suffer a countervalue attack against its cities. Such an attack would be gratuitous cruelty, and would cause immense, worldwide political harm to any country that undertook it. Also, the attack would destroy resources that a "hostile" country might wish eventually to control, and it would release radioactivity into the atmosphere that eventually would harm the attacking country.

Rather than nuclear surprise attack, the disarmed nation more likely would face blackmail threats, occupation attempts, and "nibbling" at the edges of what once had been its military zone of influence. Blackmail in the form of bombing threats would be unlikely. Making and carrying out such threats against a disarmed neighbor would be very costly politically, and less costly alternative forms of pressure would be available. In general, bombing threats could be ignored.

Occupation attempts could be countered with nonviolent resistance in the tradition established by Gandhi in India. The resistance would be characterized by noncooperation and strikes. These would be designed to raise as high as possible the psychological, political, and economic costs to the invading power.

"Nibbling" also would involve occupation attempts, and could be countered with nonviolent resistance.

Nonviolent resistance might not work perfectly, or be without risks and sacrifices. There are many historical examples that suggest that it could be effective (8), and there's no evidence whatsoever that nonviolent resistance would result in casualties and destruction more than a tiny fraction of those produced by nuclear war.

Any superpower that adopted such a program could expect a period between the program's inauguration and the establishment of world government during which world public consciousness would rise concerning the inability of military power to provide security; the anti-poverty programs were eroding the desperation and cynicism that help to generate oppression, and nonviolent resistance was raising to high levels the political costs of military aggression. The disarmed nation might have to endure occupying forces, and the distortion of normal economic processes. However, time and scientific reality would be on its side, and eventually the advantages of democratic world government, and procedures for peacefully resolving conflicts, would become universally clear.

The world government would have to be adjusted to accommodate the dominant values of the two main blocks. Its democratic and constitutional character would come from the "free world." Its economic preference probably would come from the communist and third world members. Having a world government that inclined to favor the less efficient socialist economies would be a small price to pay for freedom from the threat of nuclear war.

But why, if one or the other of the major power blocs disarmed unilaterally, would the armed bloc have to settle for a compromise? If the communists remained armed, couldn't they impose a world communist government controlled by a central committee operating under "democratic centralism" ? (9). And, if the communists unilaterally disarmed, couldn't the U.S. and its allies impose a world government that favored capitalist policies?

Strong incentives would exist to make a compromise preferable to seeking hegemony. One would be the prospect of sustained nonviolent resistance from half the world's population. Another would be the scientific realities described by the probability equations. Any nation or group of nations that was tempted to impose its will on the rest of the world would know that this could result in new nuclear arms races, and the renewed probability of nuclear war. For example, with the U.S. out of the picture, Russia and China might throw their full energies into mutual deterrence and a nuclear arms race. But, where could it lead? Only to nuclear war. The probability equations are like the law of gravity. Their predictions apply to everyone. Rather than risk such a catastrophe, all nations would be wiser to seek nonmilitary, political resolutions of their differences through a world government.

Once established, a world government would be given a monopoly of nuclear technology. This would prevent the development of antagonistic nuclear arsenals, and permit the evaluation of all applications of nuclear energy in terms of global interests.

While world government could end the immediate threat of nuclear war, it would pose dangers of its own. One would be hegemony, or domination by one interest group or another. This danger exists in all constitutional democracies, and usually has been adequately handled through constitutional guarantees of civil rights and civil liberties, executive, legislative, and judicial institutions that check and balance each other, and the creation of well-educated electorates.

World government also would permit world culture to flourish on a much greater scale than at present. There would be no competitive military institutions draining away productive resources. Science and technology could be guided to improve living conditions for the species as a whole. Environmental quality problems could be dealt with on a global scale. As science developed, the potential for weapons of ever greater destructive power would grow, always underlining the need for cooperative, global institutions, and the folly of returning to a situation dominated by antagonistic weapons systems and deterrence.

In such a situation, coercive institutions could be expected to decline within a few decades to a level representative of whatever genetic component of selfishness exists. Then, as culture continued to be characterized by institutions that de-emphasized coercion, and emphasized cooperation, the genetic composition of the entire species could be expected to change in the direction of ever lower levels of selfishness and cruelty. Once freed of its need for military force and deterrence, society would be able to develop ultimately without limit. From the time that reliance on military deterrence ended, civilization levels could be expected to progress indefinitely upward.

VI. A note on method

This paper has employed mathematical probability analysis to analyze deterrence theory and strategy. For the following reasons, I believe that this form of analysis can provide the most helpful insights.

One of the tasks of political science is to find laws that permit the prediction of the the outcome of social policies. Social phenomena are complicated, and several philosophers have claimed that neither social nor political science exists (1). Nevertheless, some progress has been made, notably in the application of statistics to election prediction and other problems, and in economics, in building a body of laws that produce reliable predictions.

There are several ways for discovering scientific laws. The most reliable is laboratory experiment. An hypothesis is formed, predictions are made, and then controlled experiments are undertaken to see if the predictions hold true. This approach is a process of elimination. It rejects hypotheses that don't produce accurate predictions. Economic programs such as the New Deal, the Marshall Plan, and "Reaganomics" are examples.

A second approach is statistical prediction. It's based on extrapolating from measurements taken of event patterns. It's appropriate when the event whose future occurrance we're curious about is very similar to the events in the pattern. Elections predictions, and Charles M. Komanoff's multivariate analysis of the comparative costs of nuclear and coal power (2), are examples.

A third approach is mathematical probability analysis. We can use it when we know that the phenomena we're studying involve risks.

A fourth approach is historical analysis. It looks at history to see if patterns of events can be perceived. It's based on the principle that, "What's happened in the past will happen in the future." Marxism is an example of this approach.

And the fifth, and least reliable technique, is intuition. It relies on "hunches" rather than on intellectual analysis. Japan's attack on Pearl Harbor, Russia's 1919 invasion of Poland, and the Bay of Pigs invasion, are examples.

All of these methods for discovering laws and making predictions have some place in political science. The problem is to use the best approach possible. The best approach is determined by the kinds of information and problems being investigated.

Nuclear deterrence is a theory about how to prevent nuclear war. Since nuclear war is an extremely important phenomenon, it's important that we investigate deterrence in the most effective manner possible.

As we've seen, most deterrence strategists have employed the historical test to evaluate deterrence: Deterrence will work because it always has worked. This test isn't the best we can apply. The test itself can be evaluated only by risking catastrophe.

We can't use the laboratory method. We can't test deterrence until it fails. It's the failure that we want to prevent.

A statistical approach isn't compelling because there're no historical examples of nuclear arms races. We can say that since most conventional arms races have ended in war, it's likely that the nuclear one will, too. But, because the nuclear arms race is different, it may not.

Intuition, "hunches", aren't reliable enough. They're too subjective.

What's left, mathematical probability analysis, is appropriate because dederrence involves risks.

VII. NOTES

iii

(1) <u>Strategy in the Missile Age</u>; Bernard Brodie; Princeton University Press; 1959; p.406

(2) <u>On Thermonuclear War</u>; Herman Kahn; Princeton University Press; 1960; pp. 33-34

(3) <u>Deterrence and Defense</u>; Glenn H. Snyder; Princeton University Press; 1961; p.16

I. Thesis

(1) From "The Evolution of American Defense Policy", by Richard Smoke, p. 94 in <u>American Defense Policy</u> (ADP) (fifth edition), ed. by John F. Reichert and Steven R. Sturm.

(2) Many probability models use the concepts of p and (1-p). To my knowledge, the only previous use of this equation in political analysis appears in a footnote at the bottom of page 1272 in Volume II of Quincy Wright's, <u>A Study of War</u>. The footnote reads:

> "The probability of war between two states during a period of time is not the product or the sum of the probabilities of war in all of the crises anticipated in their relations during the period, nor is it the probability of war in the most serious crisis. Rather it is one <u>minus</u> the probability of war being avoided during the period. This is the product of the probabilities of war being avoided in each crisis...Assume that A and B during a period of ten years passed through three crises of which the probable eventuations of war were, respectively, 50,60, and 70 percent and that states C and D had, during that period, only one crisis with a war probability of 94 per cent. It should be said, at the beginning of the period, if these probabilities were known, that the probability of the members of the two pairs being at war with each other within ten years was equal. With A and B the probability of avoiding war in the successive crises was 50, 40 and 30 percent. The product of these percentages is 6 per cent, giving a war probability of 94 per cent. If
>
> p_1, p_2, p_3 etc., indicate the probability of war in successive crises in the relations of two states and P indicates the probability of war for n crises, then
>
> $$P = 1-(1-p_1)(1-p_2)(1-p_3)\cdots(1-p_n)$$
>
> If an average probability of war is assumed for each crisis,
>
> $$P = 1-(1-p)^n$$
>
> Even though p is very small, as n approaches infinity the probability of war approaches certainty."

In 1942, when <u>A Study of War</u> was published, and nuclear weapons hadn't been developed, the equation was of little more than academic interest. Nuclear arsenals, and, particularly, recent developments in missile accuracy, have given the equation considerable importance.

(3) The equation may be derived mathematically in this way:

The event we have in mind, the accidental launching of a missile, can either occur or not occur on a given day. Let "O" indicate that it does occur, "DO" indicate that it doesn't occur. If the event does occur, then that is the end of our story. If it doesn't occur, we move to the second day. On the second day, the event can occur, or not occur. If the event doesn't occur on the second day, we move to the third day, and so on for as many days we wish ("N" days). A model of these possible events might look like this:

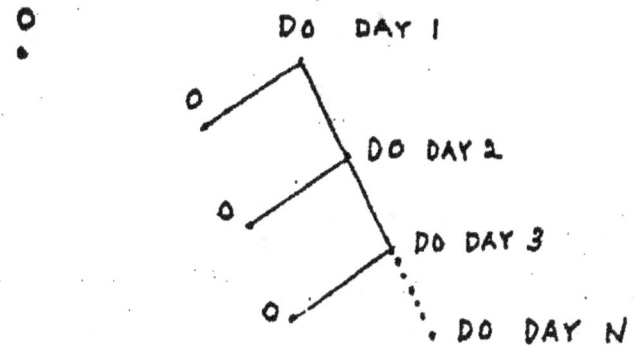

With this model in mind, let us use the letter "p" to stand for the probability that the event will happen on a given day, and the letter "q" to stand for the probability that it won't happen on a given day. The number "1" indicates a chance of 100% or certainty. Then:

$$p + q = 1$$
$$q = 1 - p$$
$$p = 1 - q$$

Now, the AP on day one is p. The AP on day two is the $q \times p$ (The accident didn't occur on day one, therefore its probability is q. We multiply $q \times p$ because the days are sequential, and the events are part of the same system.)

On day three, the AP $= q \times q \times p$, or $q^2 p$.

On the Nth day, we see that the AP would be $q^{N-1} \times p$.

But, we are interested in the total probability over all of the days. We therefore must add together the probabilities for each of the days. The mathematical symbol for adding up quantities in this way is $\sum\limits_{i=1}^{N}$ ("i" is called an "index". i=1 means that we first put 1 into our equation and evaluate the result, then 2, etc., all the way to N.) Let us use the letters "APT" to represent this accident probability over a time period of one or more days. We can write:

$$APT = \sum_{i=1}^{N} \left(q^{i-1} \times p \right)$$

Since p is in each day's calculation, we can "factor" it out and re-write our equation in this way:

$$APT = p \left[\sum_{i=1}^{N} q^{i-1} \right]$$

(We will call this "Equation #1".)

We know the value for p, but the value $\sum\limits_{i=1}^{N} q^{i-1}$ can require N calculations. However, we can simplify $\sum\limits_{i=1}^{N} q^{i-1}$ by means of the following mathematical "trick."

We know that:
$$\sum_{i=1}^{N} q^{i-1} = 1 + q + q^2 + q^3 \cdots q^{N-1}$$

And that:
$$q \left[\sum_{i=1}^{N} q^{i-1} \right] = q + q^2 + q^3 \cdots q^{N}$$

Subtracting:
$$\sum_{i=1}^{N} q^{i-1} - q \left[\sum_{i=1}^{N} q^{i-1} \right] = 1 - q^{N}$$

Factoring:
$$(1-q) \sum_{i=1}^{N} \left(q^{i-1} \right) = 1 - q^{N}$$

Dividing both sides of the equation by (1-q), we have the simplified expression that we were seeking:
$$\sum_{i=1}^{N} q^{i-1} = \frac{1 - q^{N}}{1 - q}$$

Multiplying both sides of this equation by p, we have:

$$p\left[\sum_{i=1}^{N} q^{i-1}\right] = p\left[\frac{1-q^N}{1-q}\right]$$

(We will call this "Equation #2".)

Substituting Equation #2 into Equation #1, we have:

$$APT = p\left[\frac{1-q^N}{1-q}\right]$$

Now, since $p=1-q$, then:

$$APT = (1-q)\left[\frac{1-q^N}{1-q}\right] = 1-q^N$$

And, since $q=1-p$, our final equation, that we might call "the accident probability equation, is:

$$APT = 1-(1-p)^N$$

(4) In Deterrence and Defense (Princeton University Press, 1961), Glenn H. Snyder analyzes how gain/loss considerations enter into deterrence. See particularly the models on p.17 and the subsequent discussion of them.

(5) Herman Kahn makes the distinction between authorized and unauthorized missile launches in On Thermonuclear War (Princeton University Press, 1960), p.154.

(6) Most people believe that the launches of battle-line missiles can be aborted in the same way as the test launches of military missiles, and the launches of rockets carrying satellites and astronauts. While I've found no Pentagon or SAC statements concerning this notion, there are an abundance of informal statements by government authorities and deterrence strategists implying that battle-line missile launches can't be aborted. For example, in a May 13, 1982 news conference, President Reagan said:

> "one of the reasons for going after ballistic missiles, that is the one that is the most destabilizing. That is the one that is the most frightening to most people, and let me just give you a little reasoning on that, of my own, on that score.
> That is the missile sitting there in its silo in which there could be the possibility of miscalculation. That is the one that people know that once that button is pushed there is no defense. There is no recall. And it's a matter of minutes, and the missiles reach the other country."

On page 100 in On Thermonuclear War, Herman Kahn wrote, "...The bomber has some advantages over missiles: it is recallable..."

Writing of missiles on page 19 in The Necessity for Choice, Henry A. Kissinger wrote, "Once launched, its [a missile's] flight cannot be impeded except by internal malfunctions whose frequency is statistically known..."

I can think of two reasons why battle-line missiles probably don't have

60

abort mechanisms, both due to the necessity for using coded radio signals to activate the mechanisms. One is that the codes might fall into the hands of enemy agents, who then would be able to de-activate the U.S. strategic arsenal. Another is that in wartime, the electro-magnetic pulses generated by nuclear warheads exploding nearby might activate the destruct mechanisms.

(7) The 1972 "Salt I" treaty banned all but very limited ABM systems.

(8) This problem is discussed in John Steinbruner's articles, "National Security and the Concept of Strategic Stability," published in The Journal of Conflict Resolution, Vol.22, #3, pp.411-423, and, "Nuclear Decapitation", in Foreign Policy, #45, winter 1981/82.

(9) The exponents are multiplied together. A discussion of the laws governing the probabilities relating to independent events may be found on page 19 of Engineering Statistics, A.H. Bouker & G.J. Lieberman; Prentice Hall; 1959.

(10) Actually, I've called a variation of $P = 1-(1-p)^{nm}$ the "Apocalypse Equation" (AE). In the AE, P is replaced by AP and m by (U+S), in which U represents the number of U.S. missiles, S the number of Soviet missiles. The equation then becomes: $AP = 1-(1-p)^{n(U+S)}$. Versions of the equation that aren't quite as accurate, but involve smaller exponents, are: $AP = 1-[1-p(U+S)]^{n}$, and, $AP = 1-e^{-np(U+S)}$. In the last equation, e is the natural log base 2.71828...

(11) One approach could be similar to that employed by a team of Massachusetts Institute of Technology scientists under the direction of Dr. Norman Rasmussen, to estimate the catastrophic failure probability of a nuclear power reactor. That research is reported in the Reactor Safety Study, prepared for the Nuclear Regulatory Commission, and published in 1975 (also known as The Rasmussen Report, and by its documentary code name, WASH-1400). The Rasmussen team's research cost the government about $10 million.

The problem of calculating the mechanical and electrical accident probabilities of nuclear weapons is discussed in a letter from Joel E. Cohen, "Too many nuclear weapons", in the September-October, 1981 issue of Harvard Magazine, pp.17-19.

Calculating the psychological instability of the personnel directly responsible for nuclear weapons is discussed in the monograph, "National Security Policy and Human Reliability in Military Systems", by Lloyd J. Dumas, in Papers in Science and Public Policy I; Annals of the New York Academy of Sciences; Vol.368; 1981; p.103.

(12) Appendix II consists of graphs in which curves are plotted on the basis of different assumptions concerning the value of m, the number of missiles. Appendix III shows how the curves can be used to compare different deterrence strategies.

II. A philosophic error

(1) Aristotle was aware of the problem. David Hume and Emmanual Kant analyzed it in detail. Bertrand Russell, A.J. Ayer, and Alfred North Whitehead, are modern philosophers of science who've discussed it.

III. A theory of history

(1) See George H. Quester's book, Deterrence before Hiroshima; John Wiley & Sons, NYC; 1966

(2) See the quotations from Thucydides and Bernard Brodie, pp.24-25 of this paper.

(3) The original phrase probably is Vegetius's, *"Qui desiderat pacem, para pacet bellum."*

IV. Examples

(1) Strategy in the Missile Age; Bernard Brodie; Princeton University Press; 1959.

(2) Ibid., p.216

(3) Nuclear Weapons and Foreign Policy; Henry A. Kissinger; Harper & Bros., NYC; 1957

(4) Ibid., p.116

(5) Ibid., p.173

(6) The Necessity for Choice: Prospects of American Foreign Policy; Henry A. Kissinger; Harper & Row, NYC; 1960

(7) Ibid., pp.217-218

(8) Ibid., p.424

(9) Ibid., p.436

(10) "The Delicate Balance of Terror"; Albert Wohlstetter; Foréign Affairs, January, 1959; pp.211-235

(11) Ibid., p.222

(12) Ibid., p.234

(13) Strategy in the Missile Age; Bernard Brodie; Princeton University Press; 1959

(14) Ibid., p.306

(15) Ibid., p.397

(16) "On the Objectives of Arms Control"; Bernard Brodie; International Security; pp.19-33

(17) Ibid., p.19

(18) Ibid., p.29

(19) Ibid., p.33

(20) Ibid., p.33

(21) Strategy in the Missile Age; pp.405-406

(22) On Escalation; Herman Kahn; F.A. Praeger, NYC; 1965

(23) On Thermonuclear War; p.ix. The * footnote reads:

>"Herman Kahn and Irwin Mann, Techniques of Systems Analysis, The Rand Corporation, Research Memorandum RM-1829-1, June 1957; and Ten Common Pitfalls, Research Memorandum RM-1937, July 17, 1957."

(24) Ibid., pp.33-34

(25) Ibid., pp.40-41

(26) Ibid., p.144

(27) Ibid., p.154

(28) Ibid., p.228

(29) Ibid., p.358

(30) Ibid., p.493

(31) Ibid., p.501

(32) Ibid., p.521

(33) Ibid., pp.536-537

(34) Ibid., p.574

(35) On Escalation; pp.63-64

(36) Ibid., p.226

(37) Ibid., pp.12-13

(38) Ibid., p.22

(39) Deterrence and Defense; Glenn H. Snyder; Princeton University Press; 1961

(40) Ibid., p.3

(41) Ibid., p.3

"stochastic" equations. The AE is a stochastic equation used to analyze a national policy—nuclear deterrence.

In the equation, 'p" is the probability that any given missile of the thousands that now are deployed will be launched on any one day. "T" is the period of time being considered. "N" is the number of missiles on battle-ready status (Read the exponent of the equation T times n). "AP" (for APocalyptic tragedy) is the probability over time that a missile will be launched.

There are two curves on the graph underneath the equation. Each curve is produced by a certain number of missiles. The more misiles, the greater the angle, or "slope" of the curve. The top curve is produced by the most missiles. It crosses the 50% line earlier than the bottom curve. If a perpendicular is dropped from the point where the top curve crosses the 50% line, it produces T_1. A perpendicular dropped from the point where the bottom curve crosses the 50% line produces T_2. Since OT_1 is less than OT_2, the graph shows that increasing the number of missiles in strategic arsenals shortens the time before a missile launch becomes probable. More missiles make nuclear apocalypse more likely.

The AE shows that, given antagonistic nuclear missile systems, the probability of thermonuclear accidents and thermonuclear war approaches certainty. Nuclear deterrence is a "Faustian bargain," that may generate "peace" for an indeterminate period, but only at the cost of eventual, catastrophic nuclear accidents and attacks.

Still another insight that the equation provides is how safe nuclear missile arsenals must be if we are to live with them for any significant period. This safety factor is found in "p." p is made up of many factors, including the mechanical reliability fo the missiles, and the psychological stability fo the crews controlling them. If it is assumed that p is as small as one chance in one-hundred-million (10^{-8}) and there are 4,000 strategic nuclear missiles in the arsenals of the nuclear powers, then it can be calculated by means of the equation that in 50 years the probability of the launch of at least one missile is about 52%. Even if the daily chance of an accidental launch is astronomically small, some missile probably will be launched within a relatively short time.

Since nuclear weapons are the ultimate expression of military force, the AE shows that the ultimate consequence of attempting found "civilization" on military force is catastrophic nuclear war.

Our reliance on military force has other destructive consequences. Military institutions and weapons are impoverishing us. Even in the richest nation on earth, we now are choosing to reduce health care, education, and other needed services in order to maintain and even increase giant military systems. Also, in order to strengthen our military posture, we often make alliances with totalitarian and corrupt government. And, we find ourselves frequently tempted to employ torture to extract information that we believe may give us an advantage in military conflicts.

Since military systems always are justified on the grounds that they are necessary to defend freedom and promote justice, the key question before the human species is how these values can be achieved and defended without military force. Nonviolent resistance is the answer proposed by Mohandas Gandhi, Martin Luther King, and other humanitarian leaders. Part of nonviolent resistance are worldwide programs to create economic and social justice, and overcome poverty and all forms of racial, sexual, social, and religious discrimination.

For more information about nonviolent resistance and international peacemaking efforts:
Midwest Pacifist Center, 5729 S. Dorchester Ave., Chicago, IL 60637; Tel: 773.324.0654; Fax: 773.324.6426; Email: byttle@igc.org , or United States Pacifist Party, http://www.uspacifistparty.org

Appendix 3

A scientific analysis of the probability of war between nation states can be achieved by the mathematical analysis of probability over time, technically called "stochastic" analysis. Stochastic analysis is widely used in physics, astronomy, chemistry, biology, the insurance industry, and many other fields. As far as I know, its first use in political science appears on page 1272 (see below) of Quincy Wright's A Study of War, a two volume, 1552 page work published by the University of Chicago Press in 1942. Quincy Wright was professor of international law at the University of Chicago 1923-1956, president of the American Political Science Association 1948-49, and president of the American Association of University Professors 1943-45.

indicating the gravity of successive crises, a persistent pattern might emerge. The probability of war between two states during a period of time is a function of the number of crises and the probability of avoiding war in each crisis.[38]

A short political cycle of four or five years is suggested by the usual life of a political administration in most countries and the average duration of a war between great powers.[39] A longer political cycle of from forty to sixty years has also been suggested by the average dominance of a political party in democratic countries and by the periodicity of general wars during epochs dominated by an expanding economy and a balance-of-power system. The tendency to postpone a new war until there has been time to recover economically from the last, coupled with the waning resistance to a new war as social memory of the last one fades with the passage of a generation, may influence this tendency toward periodicity.[40]

Even longer periods of from two to three centuries have been detected, marking the phases of the development of a civilization, and

[38] The probability of war between two states during a period of time is not the product or the sum of the probabilities of war in all of the crises anticipated in their relations during the period, nor is it the probability of war in the most serious crisis. Rather it is one *minus* the probability of war being avoided during the period. This is the product of the probabilities of war being avoided in each crisis (see above, n. 17). Assume that A and B during a period of ten years passed through three crises of which the probable eventuations in war were, respectively, 50, 60, and 70 per cent and that states C and D had, during that period, only one crisis with a war probability of 94 per cent. It should be said, at the beginning of the period, if these probabilities were known, that the probability of the members of the two pairs being at war with each other within ten years was equal. With A and B the probability of avoiding war in the successive crises was 50, 40, and 30 per cent. The product of these percentages is 6 per cent, giving a war probability of 94 per cent. If p_1, p_2, p_3, etc., indicate the probability of war in successive crises in the relations of two states and P indicates the probability of war for n crises, then

$$P = 1 - (1 - p_1)(1 - p_2)(1 - p_3) \ldots (1 - p_n).$$

If an average probability of war is assumed for each crisis,

$$P = 1 - (1 - p)^n.$$

Even though p is very small, as n approaches infinity the probability of war approaches certainty.

[39] Above, Vol. I, chap. ix, sec. 2c. Richardson suggests that a three-year period is necessary both for rearmament and for disarmament (see below, Appen. XLII, nn. 8 and 9).

[40] Above, Vol. I, chap. ix, sec. 2d.

(42) Ibid., p.12

(43) Ibid., pp.100-101

(44) Arms and Influence; Thomas C. Schelling; Yale University Press; New Haven, Ct.; 1966

(45) Ibid., p.92

(46) Ibid., pp.94-95

(47) Ibid., pp.93-94

(48) Ibd., p.94

(49) Ibid., pp.96-97

(50) Ibid., p.98

(51) Ibid., p.99

(52) Ibid., p.109

(53) Ibid., p.113

(54) Ibid., p.248

(55) Ibid., p.248

(56) "Arms Races: Prerequisites and Results"; Samuel P. Huntington; The Use of Force; Art & Watty

(57) Ibid., p.520

(58) Ibid., p.512

(59) "What Deters? The Ability to Inflict Assured Destruction"; Robert Jervis; ADP; pp.161-170

(60) Ibid., p.169

(61) Ibid., p.169

(62) Deterrence; Patrick M. Morgan; Vol.40 of Sage Library of Social Research; Sage Pubs., Beverly Hills, Ca.

(63) Ibid., p.9

(64) Ibid., p.47

(65) Ibid., pp.214-215

(66) Ibid., p.14

(67) Ibid., p.36

(68) "Strategic Deterrence Reconsidered", Richard Rosecrance; The International Institute for Strategic Studies; London; Paper #116; 1975. On microfilm at Regenstein Library, University of Chicago

(69) The New York Times; April 13, 1982; op ed page

(70) The New York Times; April 7, 1982; p.6

(71) Ibid., p.15

(72) Ibid., p.16

(73) The MX ICBM and National Security; Colin S. Gray; Praeger; 1982; p.95

(74) Ibid., p.4

(75) Ibid., p.97

(76) Ibid., p.58

V. Conclusions

(1) The MX ICBM; p.106

(2) Pencil and paper approximations can be made by means of the binomial theorem. As previously mentioned, the calculations are easily made on a pocket calculator that has appropriate functions. A micro-computer will do the job, too. Appendix I is an article that includes Apocalypse Equation programs for an Apple computer.

(3) See Gray's "What Deters/ The Ability to Wage Nuclear War", ADP, pp.171-187, and The MX ICBM and National Security (Praeger, 1982), and Pipes's, "Why The Soviet Union Thinks It Could Fight and Win a Nuclear War," Commentary, July, 1977, pp.21-34.

(4) In recent years, the Scientific American has carried a number of articles about weapons systems, that bear this out. Authors have included Kosta Tsipis and Bernard Feld.

(5) Bernard Brodie and Herman Kahn are among the military historians who've noted this.

(6) See Kosta Tsipis's article,"Laser Weapons", in the Dec., 1981 issue of Scientific American; pp.51-57.

(7) Nietsche, who believed that people are basically cruel, is among the political philosophers in this tradition.

(8) The most comprehensive historical study of nonviolence is Gene Sharp's The Politics of Nonviolent Action (Extending Horizon Books, Boston, MA; 1973).

(9) The Leninist/Stalinist term to describe the decision-making process in Russia and the Communist Party.

VI. A note on method

(1) Among the philosophers who've contributed to this perspective are Stanislav Andreski in Social Science as Scorcery (1972), Alfred Schutz in The Phenomenology of the Social World (1932), and Peter Winch in The Idea of a Social Science and its Relation to Philosophy (1958).

(2) See A Comparison of Nuclear and Coal Costs; Charles Komanoff Energy Associates, 475 Park Ave., South, 32nd floor, NYC 10016; 1978.

For stochastic theory see also "Stochastic Problems in Physics and Astronomy;" Subramanyan Chandrasekhar; Jan. 1943 ed. of Reviews of Modern Physics

CREATIVE COMPUTING
May, 1983

The Apocalypse Equations

Howard S. Balsam

The last book of the Bible is that of Revelation or Apocalypse. It describes the end of this world with the Battle of Armageddon and the advent of the next and perfect world. Engendered by the growth of nuclear weaponry over the last 35 years and by massive and skillful Kremlin-fanned propaganda, there is a widespread fear of starting Armageddon by accidentally launching an armed nuclear missile from either the United States or Soviet Russia.

In the *Harvard Magazine* for March/April, 1982 appeared a letter by one Bradford Lyttle, of Chicago, presenting three forms of an equation which he says gives the probability of such an accidental Armageddon. The Apocalypse program, which follows, presents these equations so you may investigate the presumed probability of Apocalypse.

Probability is often expressed as a decimal between zero and one. A probability near zero indicates that the chances of a given event ocurring are considered very low. A probability near one says that the chances are very high that the event will occur. Probabilities exceeding about 0.95 are often considered practically certain. Probability is expressed as a percentage in this program: 100% = 1.00, a certainty.

The Equations

The three equations use these symbols:

AP is the Probability of Apocalypse, that is, the probability over a period of time that the accidental launch of one nuclear missile by either the United States or the Soviet Union would falsely trigger a nuclear World War III.

Howard S. Balsam, 104 Appleside Drive, Nashua, NH 03060.

U is the total number of strategic missiles in the U.S. arsenal. The program suggests 1900. You may wish to adjust this.

S is the total number of strategic missiles in the Soviet arsenal. The program suggests 2200; again, you may adjust this value.

P is the probability of the accidental launching of an armed strategic nuclear missile by either the U.S. or the Soviet Union during any 24-hour period. The program suggests that there is one

Run the program and find out what the future holds—if anything.

chance in one hundred million of this: 1E-8. Change this if desired.

N is the number of days in the period considered. You may enter whatever period you wish: the program suggests 14,600 days—40 years. You may consider that the clock started ticking perhaps 20 years ago, with a much smaller number of missiles.

The three equations given by Mr. Lyttle are:

Approximate:
$$AP = 1-(1-P(U+S))^N$$

Closer approximation:
$$AP = 1-e^{(-NP(U+S))}$$

Exact Form:
$$AP = 1-(1-P)^{N(U+S)}$$

It turns out that the values given by the first two equations are usually very close to one another, while the exact equation gives a slightly smaller value.

Program Structure

The Applesoft program consists of 14 sections or routines ranging from 1 to 12 lines each in length. In approximate order of operation, the main routines are:

    1000-1090 Introduction
    800- 890 Menu
    600- 720 Entries
    300- 370 Approximate Equation
    400- 470 Closer Approximation
    500- 570 Exact Equation
    140- 180 Results

Brief routines handle such operations as centering phrases on the screen, rounding numbers, rejecting out-of-line values, and beeping three times. The Entries subroutine is designed to minimize number re-entries; after the initial entries, each re-entry with the same value can be made with one keystroke. The program is fairly well bullet-proofed and includes many REMarks.

Variations

While the program considers strategic missiles of the U.S. and Soviet Russia only, the nuclear "club" is growing. You may modify the program accordingly.

You may wish to take a short-cut, at least for a minimum-effort trial. If so, try skipping lines 1000-1090 (Introduction).

If you do this, make line 10 read: GOTO 810. Of course, you may also omit the REMs. If you find the beeps annoying, delete lines 70-80 and GOSUB 80 in lines 200, 350, 450, 550, 890 and 1100.

Now, RUN the program and find out what the future holds—if anything. □

```
10 GOTO 1010: REM GO FOR INTRO.
20 REM BY HOWARD S. BALSAM.
30 REM < ROUNDING ROUTINE >
40 X1 = 100 * X1% : INT (X1 * 100 + .5) / 100: RETURN
50 REM < CENTERING ROUTINE >
60 HTAB ((40 - LEN (T$)) / 2 + 1): PRINT T$: RETURN
70 REM < BEEP ROUTINE >
80 CALL - 198: CALL - 198: PRINT T$: RETURN
90 REM <CONTINUATION ROUTINE>
100 PRINT "HIT ANY KEY TO CONTINUE ";: GET Z$: PRINT T$: RETURN
140 REM < RESULTS ROUTINE >
150 IF A1 THEN PRINT "APPROXIMATE PROBABILITY IS
160 IF A2 THEN PRINT PRINT "CLOSER APPROXIMATION IS
170 IF A3 THEN PRINT PRINT "EXACT PROBABILITY IS
180 RETURN
190 REM < REJECTION ROUTINE >
200 INVERSE : PRINT "PLEASE ENTER A MORE REALISTIC VALUE. ": GOSUB 80: FOR
    T = 1 TO 1500: NEXT T: NORMAL : VTAB VT + 1: CALL - 958: RETURN : REM
    DISPLAY REJECTION FOR READING, BEEPS, MOVE UP AND CLEAR SCREEN BELOW
299 REM < THREE FORMS OF EQ. >
300 HOME : T$ = "<A> APPROXIMATE FORM": GOSUB 60: PRINT
310 HTAB 12: PRINT "AP = 1 - CHR$ (91)"1-F(U+S)J^N": PRINT
320 GOSUB 620: REM GO FOR ENTRIES.
340 A1 = 1 - (1 - P *(U + S)) ^ N
350 X = A1: GOSUB 40:A1 = X: REM PER CENT AND ROUNDING.
360 PRINT : GOSUB 150: GOSUB 80: PRINT : REM DISPLAY RESULTS, WITH 3 BEE
    PS.
370 GOTO 810: REM BACK TO MENU.
400 HOME : T$ = "<C> CLOSER APPROXIMATION": GOSUB 60: PRINT
410 T$ = "AP = 1-EXP(-NF(U+S))": GOSUB 60: PRINT
420 GOSUB 620: REM GO FOR ENTRIES.
430 A2 = 1 - EXP ( - N * P * (U + S))
440 X = A2: GOSUB 40:A2 = X: REM PER CENT AND ROUNDING.
450 PRINT : GOSUB 150: GOSUB 80: PRINT : REM DISPLAY RESULTS, WITH 3 BEE
    PS.
460 GOTO 810: REM BACK TO MENU.
470 HOME : T$ = "<E> EXACT EQUATION": GOSUB 60: PRINT
500 T$ = "AP = 1-(1-F) ^ N(U+S)": GOSUB 60: PRINT
510 GOSUB 620: REM GO FOR ENTRIES.
520 A3 = 1 - (1 - P) ^ (N * (U + S))
530 X = A3: GOSUB 40:A3 = X: REM PER CENT AND ROUNDING.
540 PRINT : GOSUB 150: GOSUB 80: PRINT : REM DISPLAY RESULTS, WITH 3 BEE
    PS.
550 GOTO 810: REM BACK TO MENU.
560 PRINT : PRINT : GOSUB 100
570 GOTO 810: REM BACK TO MENU.
600 REM < ENTRIES ROUTINE >
610 REM UZ, SZ, PZ, AND NZ ARE FLAGS INDICATING NEW (0) OR CHANGED (0) EN
    TRIES OF THE RESPECTIVE QUANTITIES. 1 = NO CHANGE.
620 UZ = 0: IF U THEN PRINT "IS U="; U; " US MISSILES OK?"
630 VT = PEEK (37): PRINT A$: IF A$ = "Y" THEN UZ = 1: GOTO 640
    1900): PRINT "ENTER NO. OF US MISSILES: ": INPUT "(POSSIBLE!
    200: PRINT VT: PRINT : IF U < 1000 OR U > 5000 THEN GOSUB
640 SZ = 0: IF S THEN PRINT "IS S=" SOVIET MISSILES OK?": HTAB 32: PRINT
    "Y/N ";: GET A$: PRINT A$: IF A$ = "Y" THEN SZ = 1: GOTO 660
650 VT = PEEK (37): PRINT "ENTER NO. OF SOVIET MISSILES: ": INPUT "(POSSIB
    LE! 2200):
    200: GOTO 650
```

```
660 PZ = 0: IF P THEN PRINT "IS P= "P" ACCIDENTAL LAUNCH": HTAB 12: PRINT
    "PROBABILITY OK?";: PRINT "Y/N ";: GET A$: PRINT A$: IF A$ =
    "Y" THEN PZ = 1: GOTO 680
670 VT = PEEK (37): PRINT "ENTER CHANCE OF ACCIDENTAL LAUNCH OF ": PRINT
    "ANY GIVEN MISSILE OVER ANY 24-HR PERIOD": INPUT "(POSSIBLE! 1E-8):
    "; P: IF P < 1E - 12 OR P > 1E - 3 THEN GOSUB 200: GOTO 6
    70
680 NZ = 0: IF N THEN PRINT "IS N= "N" DAYS OK?": HTAB 32: PRINT "Y/N ";
    : GET A$: PRINT A$: IF A$ = "Y" THEN NZ = 1: GOTO 700
690 VT = PEEK (37): PRINT : PRINT "ENTER NUMBER OF DAYS:": INPUT "(POSSIB
    LE! 14600):
    200: GOTO 690
700 FLZ = UZ + SZ + NZ: REM FLAG INDICATING WHETHER ALL OR SOME CHAN
    GES MADE.
710 IF FLZ = > 4 THEN A1 = 0:A2 = 0:A3 = 0: REM IF ANY CHANGES, SUPPRESS
    PREVIOUS RESULTS IN LINES 150-170, READY FOR NEW RESULTS.
720 RETURN
800 REM < MENU ROUTINE >
810 HOME : T$ = "THE APOCALYPSE EQUATION": GOSUB 60: PRINT T$ = "HERE ARE
    3 FORMS OF THE EQUATION.": GOSUB 60:T$ = "READY FOR USE.": GOSUB 60:
    PRINT
820 HTAB 10: PRINT "<A> ALGEBRAIC FORM": HTAB 10: PRINT "<C> CLOSER APPRO
    XIMATION": PRINT
830 HTAB 10: PRINT "<E> EXACT FORM": HTAB 10: PRINT "<Q> QUIT": PRINT : PRINT
840 VT = PEEK (37) + 1: PRINT "WHICH IS YOUR CHOICE?";: GET Z$: REM VT
    = CURRENT VERT SCREEN POSITION.
850 IF Z$ = "Q" THEN 1100
860 IF Z$ = "A" THEN 300
870 IF Z$ = "C" THEN 400
880 IF Z$ = "E" THEN 500
890 VTAB VT: HTAB 1: CALL - 868: GOTO 840: REM IF NOT VALID CHOICE, MOVE
    BACK UP, CLEAR LINE, RE-QUESTION.
1000 REM < INTRODUCTION >
1010 TEXT : HOME : POKE 34,2:T$ = "THE 'APOCALYPSE EQUATION'": INVERSE : GOSUB 60: NORMAL
     : PRINT : PRINT : GOSUB 60: PRINT : GOSUB 60: PRINT ; FROM A ": GOSUB 6
1020 T$ = "LETTER FROM BRADFORD LYTTLE, CHICAGO,": GOSUB 60
1030 T$ = "IN 'HARVARD MAGAZINE,' MAR-APR 1982.": GOSUB 60:T$ = "EQUATIONS
     0:!T$ = "PAGE 19, THE AUTHOR PRESENTS THREE": GOSUB 60
     WHICH HE SAYS GIVE THE": GOSUB 60:T$ = "PROBABILITY OF AN ACCIDENTAL
     EXPLOSION": GOSUB 60:T$ = "OF A NUCLEAR WEAPON OVER TIME.": GOSUB 60
1040 T$ = "HE SPECIFICALLY DEALS WITH THE": GOSUB 60:T$ = "CHANCE OF THE A
     CCIDENTAL LAUNCH OF A": GOSUB 60:T$ = "STRATEGIC MISSILE, CONSIDERING
     ONLY THE": GOSUB 60:T$ = "U.S. AND THE USSR.": GOSUB 60
1050 PRINT :T$ = "IT IS PRESUMED THAT SUCH AN ACCIDENT": GOSUB 60:T$ = "W
     OULD TRIGGER THE APOCALYPSE.": GOSUB 60
1060 PRINT :T$ = "YOU MAY PLAY WITH THESE EQUATIONS,": GOSUB 60:T$ = "COM
     PARING THEIR RESULTS WITH EACH OTHER": GOSUB 60:T$ = "AND WITH GOD'S
     REAL WORLD.": GOSUB 60: PRINT : GOSUB 100
1070 HOME :T$ = "SYMBOLS USED:": PRINT : GOSUB 60: PRINT : PRINT "AF = FR
     OBABILITY OF APOCALYPSE": PRINT "(I.E., PROBABILITY THAT ACCIDENTAL
     "LAUNCH OF 1 MISSILE WOULD FALSELY ", "TRIGGER A FULL-FLEDGED NUCLEAR
     WAR.")"
1080 PRINT : PRINT "U = NO. U.S. MISSILES": PRINT : PRINT "S = NO. SOVIET
     MISSILES": PRINT
1090 PRINT "P = PROBABILITY OF ACCIDENTAL LAUNCH", " OF ANY MISSILE IN
     A 24-HOUR PERIOD": PRINT : PRINT "N = NO. OF DAYS IN TOTAL PERIOD",
     CONSIDERED": PRINT : PRINT : GOSUB 100: GOTO 810
1100 PRINT :T$ = "END OF 'APOCALYPSE'.": GOSUB 60: GOSUB 80: TEXT : VTAB
     20: END
```

68

Appendix II.   AP Curve Calculation Sheet

The equation used is:

$$P_m = 10^{-8} \qquad y = 1 - P_m(U+S) \qquad AP = 1 - \left[1 - P_m(U+S)\right]^n$$

Years	h(days)	6,000 y=.99994	4,000 y=.99996	2,000 y=.99998	1,000 y=.99999	500 y=.999995
1	365	.0217	.0145	.0073	.0036	.0018
5	1825	.1051	.0704	.0358	.0181	.0091
10	3650	.1967	.1358	.0704	.0358	.0181
15	5475	.2800	.1967	.1037	.0532	.0270
20	7300	.3547	.2532	.1358	.0704	.0358
25	9125	.4216	.3058	.1668	.0872	.0446
30	10956	.4816	.3547	.1967	.1037	.0533
35	12775					
40	14600	.5836	.4423	.2532	.1358	.0704
45	16425					
50	18250	.6655	.5181	.3058	.1668	.0872
55	20075					
60	21900	.7313	.5836	.3547	.1967	.1036
65	23725					
70	25550	.7841	.6401	.4011	.2255	.1199
75	27375					
80	29200	.8266	.6870	.4423	.2532	.1358
85	31025					
90	32850	.8607	.7313	.4816	.2800	.1515
95	34675					
100	36500	.8881	.7678	.5181	.3058	.1668
110	40150	.9101	.7993	.5520	.3307	.1819
120	43800					
130	47450	.9420	.8501	.6129	.3778	.2112
140	51100					
150	54750	.9626	.8881	.6655	.4216	.2375
160	58400					
170	62050	.9758	.9164	.7109	.4623	.2667
180	65700					
190	69350					
200	73000	.9875	.9761	.7678	.5181	.3058

GRAPH #1 (90 Years)
$P_m = 10^{-8}$

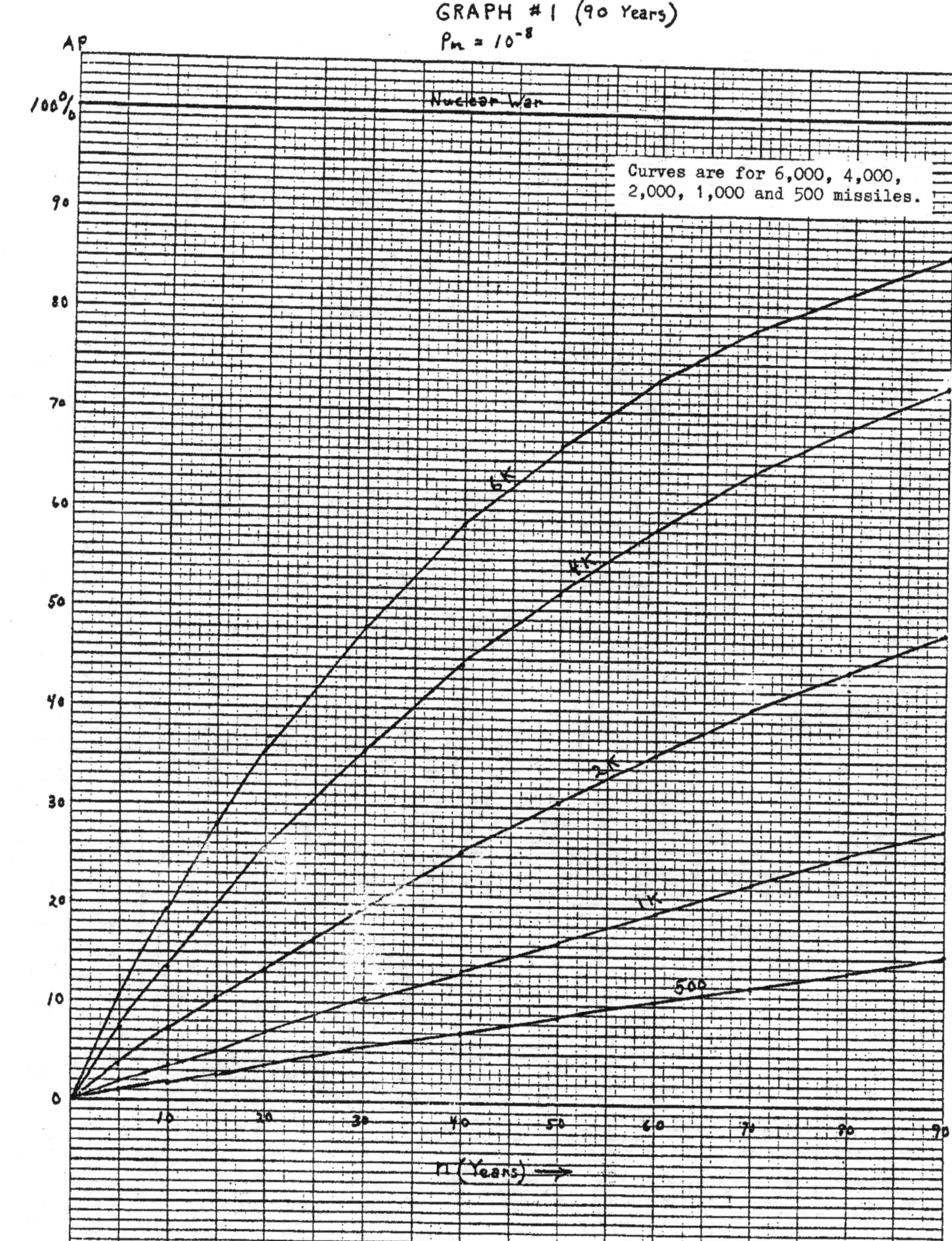

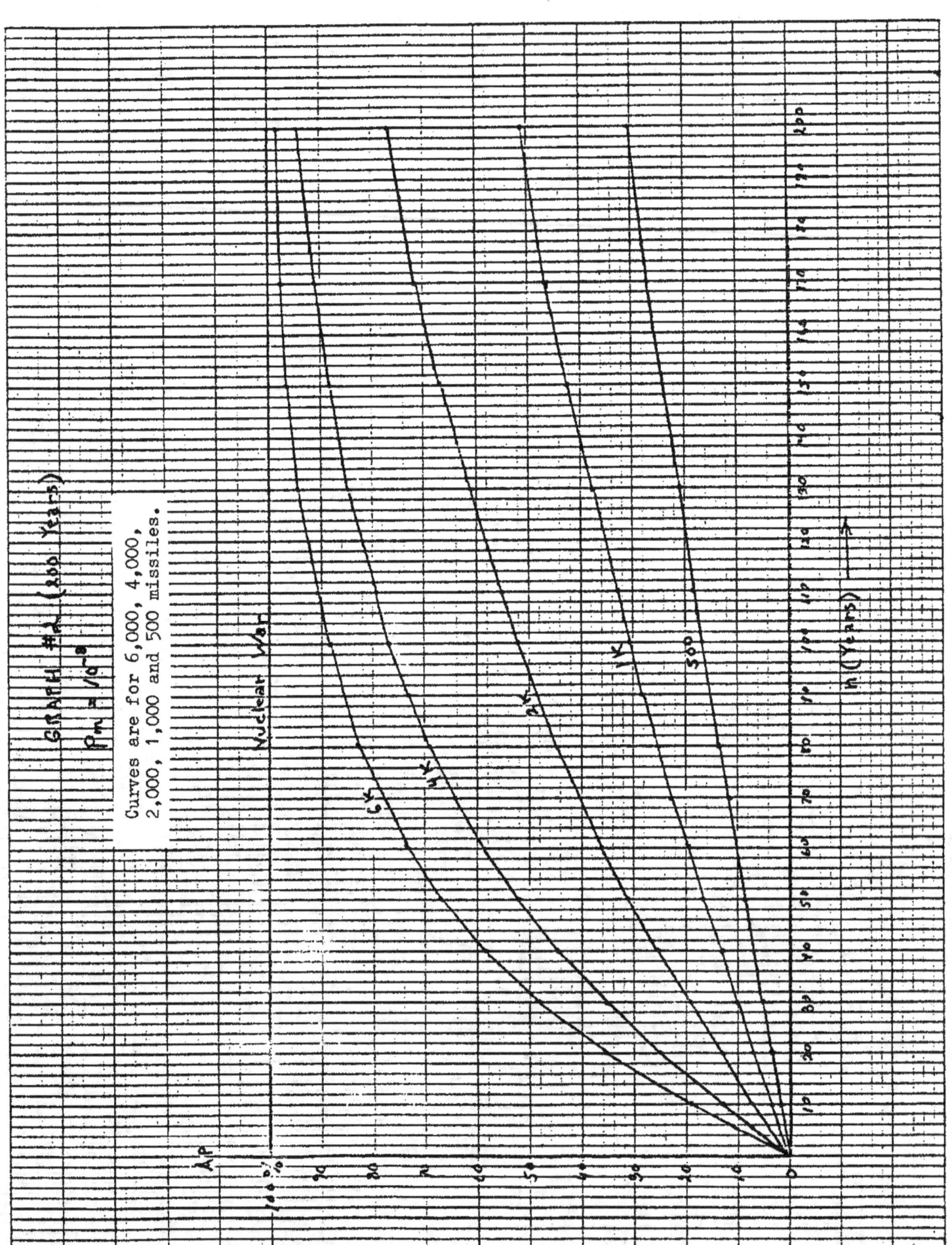

GRAPH #2 (200 Years)

$P_m = /q^{-8}$

Curves are for 6,000, 4,000, 2,000, 1,000 and 500 missiles.

Nuclear War

M (Years) ⟶

71

Appendix III.

THE APOCALYPSE EQUATION

$$AP = 1 - (1-p)^{n(U+S)}$$

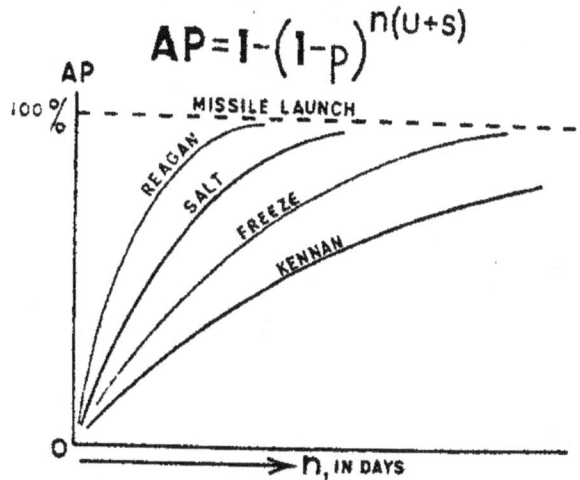

Unauthorized missile launch curves comparing
different deterrence strategies. President
Reagan proposes to increase the number of U.S.
missiles. George F. Kennan has suggested
halving the U.S. arsenal.

SUPPLEMENTARY APPENDICES

Appendix 1.

From <u>Harvard Magazine</u>

1. "The Apocalypse Equation." <u>Harvard Magazine</u>, March-April 1982, pp. 19-20.

2. From the Letters section. <u>Harvard Magazine,</u> July-August 1982, pp. 18-21.

Appendix 2.

"The Enola Gay and the Apocalypse Equation." A leaflet distributed in 1995 at the Enola Gay

Exhibit, National Air and Space Museum, Washington, D.C.

Appendix 3.

From Quincy Wright's <u>A Study of War.</u> Chicago: University of Chicago Press, 1942. Page 1272.

Appendix 4.

"The Name of the Game" by Bradford Lyttle, September 29, 1997.

Appendix 5.

"Nuclear War is Inevitable—Unless...", by Martin Hellman. <u>Parade Magazine</u>, August 24, 1986.

page 17.

Appendix 1

From HARVARD MAGAZINE
March-April 1982
Pp.19-20

The Apocalypse Equation

In his essay in the September-October issue ("Too many nuclear weapons," page 17). Joel E. Cohen has rightly pointed out that the possibility of the accidental explosion of a nuclear weapon may pose a substantial danger to humanity. While his statistical analysis is a valuable contribution to the subject of nuclear-weapons accidents, further insights into the seriousness of the problem can be gained from mathematical equations that accurately give the probability of an accident over a period of time. Generically, these equations may be called Apocalypse Equations (AE).

To explain them, we might consider the chance of the accidental launch of a strategic missile. A form of the AE that lends itself to simple algebra is:

$$AP = 1 - [1 - p (U+S)]^n$$

where AP = the probability of an accidental launch of a nuclear missile over a period of time; p = the chance of the accidental launch of any given missile over any 24-hour period; U = the number of United States missiles; S = the number of Soviet missiles, and n = the number of days. To show how the equation works, let's say that we want to know the chance of an accident over a one-year period. Then $n = 365$ (days); $U = 2,000$ (approximately); $S = 2,000$ (approximately); and we don't know the exact value of p, but let's assume it's very, very small, like 10^{-8}, or one chance in one hundred million.

Inserting these values into the AE we find that the likelihood of an accidental launch in one year is 1.4 percent. In forty years, the likelihood is more than fifty percent.

Since there have been thousands of missiles in place for more than a decade, the equation already has been "working" for some time.

The value of p is the only factor we don't have the data to approximate. It may be argued that p is much smaller than 10^{-8}. On the other hand, it may be larger. Probably p could be calculated for missiles in much the same way as a team of M.I.T. scientists, under the leadership of Norman Rasmussen, has calculated the probability of a nuclear-reactor accident. The data about missile design and control that would make possible a calculation of p probably exists in military files.

It's obvious that the value of p is of vital importance to the human species, for it enables us to calculate how much time we likely have to stop the arms race and abolish nuclear weapons. People concerned about this matter, therefore, should demand that the governments of the United States and the Soviet Union, and other countries that have nuclear missiles, make public the data for calculating p.

The form of the AE given produces a close approximation. A closer approximation can be reached by the equation $AP = 1 - e^{-np(U+S)}$, where $e = 2.71828$. An equation that produces an exact result is $AP = 1 - (1-p)^{n(U+S)}$.

The concept of p can be varied to mean the possibility of an accidental nuclear-warhead explosion. In this case, $U + S = 50,000$.

All these equations produce logarithmic curves that approach certainty, and have a number of political implications. They show why increasing the number of missiles increases the likelihood of an accidental missile launch, and at least in that respect is not in the interest of the country. They also show why there is more to the problem of preventing nuclear war than just keeping irresponsible fingers off the "nuclear trigger." That's important, but as long as the missile systems exist, the chance of a catastrophic accident approaches certainty, no matter whose finger is on the trigger. For these reasons, nuclear "containment" is a policy that may work in the short run, but in a few decades is likely to produce catastrophic accidents that could result in nuclear war.

The equations can be given a religious interpretation. Nuclear-missile systems have made it possible to statistically predict an apocalyptic event. An insight into the potential magnitude of the event can be gained by considering the destructive power of a Trident submarine, which within twenty minutes can launch 406 nuclear bombs, each of which has an explosive power ten times that of the bomb that destroyed Hiroshima. The U.S. plans to have thirteen of these submarines on station soon. Presumably the Soviet Union will have its own fleet of equally destructive submarines.

When he was in the United States recently to receive the 1981 Franklin Medal, Stephen Hawking, the noted British astrophysicist, had this to say about accidental war:

Even if the probability of war occurring by mistake or miscalculation is low in any one year, the cumulative probability over the next hundred years is frighteningly high.

This is by far the most fundamental problem facing our civilization, and it is of much more importance than any political issues that divide us. We should press for immediate disarmament, unilaterally if necessary. We do not want a future archaeologist from another star to record that the human race destroyed itself over an argument about the economic organization of production or over a few square miles of territory.

BRADFORD LYTTLE

Chicago

(over)

www.ingramcontent.com/pod-product-compliance
Lightning Source LLC
Chambersburg PA
CBHW081557280526
45788CB00011B/3495

THE NAME OF THE GAME

by Bradford Lyttle
Ver. 9/29/97

Contrary to what many people might expect, pacifism is compatible with the most modern branches of political science. This can be demonstrated by showing how "rational choice theory," "game theory," and probability analysis, three fields of political science theorizing, fit together to demonstrate that pacifism's the most reasonable and scientific approach to international relations.

Both rational choice and game theory are based on classical economic analysis, and make use of a concept called "utility." Utility is a way of expressing a person's degree of preference. For example, if a person prefers lentils to steak, would say that for that person, lentils have more utility than steak. If we let U_l represent the preference for the lentils, and U_s the preference for the steak, then the preference for the lentils over the steak can be expressed symbolically this way:

$$U_l > U_s$$

Also, we can express the preference by assigning numbers to the preferences. For example, we could say that the number 5 represents the person's preference for the lentils, and the number 3 the preference for the steak. This numerical way of comparing utilities can be tricky, for it tempts one to treat utilities as if they can be precisely measured, and manipulated in all the ways that mathematics manipulates numbers. Doing this doesn't always make sense. For our purposes, we'll limit the use of numbers to simply show that a person has one preference that's greater than another.

Rational choice theory tells us that a choice is always rational if a person, when comparing utilities, always chooses the higher utility. For example, if the person who likes lentils better than steak always chooses the lentils, then he or she is acting rationally. Choosing the steak over the lentils would be irrational. This definition of a rational choice must be modified by a notion of "reality." A mentally ill person might prefer to believe him or herself to be Napoleon rather than Julius Caesar, but because neither idea has a strong relationship to reality we wouldn't call it rational even if the person always tried to act like Napoleon.

Game theory is a branch of rational choice theory. Game theory has to do with situations in which a person's choices are reactions to what he or she thinks another person will do. A situation called "prisoners' dilemma" (pd) strikingly illustrates game theory, and is the subject of a great deal of modern political science theorizing.

In prisoner's dilemma, a district attorney has had arrested and imprisoned incommunicado in respect to each other two people suspected of conspiracy in a crime. The d.a. then goes to each prisoner, and offers him or her a "deal." If the prisoner confesses, he or she will receive a small sentence. If he or she doesn't confess, and the d.a. wins the case, the d.a. will ask for the maximum sentence. The prisoners also know if that if neither of them confesses there's a good chance that they'll go free. What will each prisoner do? Each knows that if both keep quiet, if they "cooperate" with each other, they may go free. However, neither knows that the other will decide to do that. Both also know that if he or she decides to "defect" and confess, he or she probably will receive a short sentence. But both also know that if they don't confess, and the other does, he or she will receive the maximum sentence. It's to the self-interest of the two to cooperate with each other and not confess, but since neither knows what the other will do, the most rational course is to confess. Consequently, both defect and confess.

This situation can be symbolized by the following "matrix," where:

"c" means to cooperate with the other prisoner and keep silent;

"d" means to defect and confess;

"#1=3" means that for prisoner #1, the

1

THE NAME OF THE GAME

by Bradford Lyttle
Ver. 9/29/97

Contrary to what many people might expect, pacifism is compatible with the most modern branches of political science. This can be demonstrated by showing how "rational choice theory," "game theory," and probability analysis, three fields of political science theorizing, fit together to demonstrate that pacifism's the most reasonable and scientific approach to international relations.

Both rational choice and game theory are based on classical economic analysis, and make use of a concept called "utility." Utility is a way of expressing a person's degree of preference. For example, if a person prefers lentils to steak, would say that for that person, lentils have more utility than steak. If we let U_l represent the preference for the lentils, and U_s the preference for the steak, then the preference for the lentils over the steak can be expressed symbolically this way:

$$U_l > U_s$$

Also, we can express the preference by assigning numbers to the preferences. For example, we could say that the number 5 represents the person's preference for the lentils, and the number 3 the preference for the steak. This numerical way of comparing utilities can be tricky, for it tempts one to treat utilities as if they can be precisely measured, and manipulated in all the ways that mathematics manipulates numbers. Doing this doesn't always make sense. For our purposes, we'll limit the use of numbers to simply show that a person has one preference that's greater than another.

Rational choice theory tells us that a choice is always rational if a person, when comparing utilities, always chooses the higher utility. For example, if the person who likes lentils better than steak always chooses the lentils, then he or she is acting rationally. Choosing the steak over the lentils would be irrational. This definition of a rational choice must be modified by a notion of "reality." A mentally ill person might prefer to believe him or herself to be Napoleon rather than Julius Caesar, but because neither idea has a strong relationship to reality we wouldn't call it rational even if the person always tried to act like Napoleon.

Game theory is a branch of rational choice theory. Game theory has to do with situations in which a person's choices are reactions to what he or she thinks another person will do. A situation called "prisoners' dilemma" (pd) strikingly illustrates game theory, and is the subject of a great deal of modern political science theorizing.

In prisoner's dilemma, a district attorney has had arrested and imprisoned incommunicado in respect to each other two people suspected of conspiracy in a crime. The d.a. then goes to each prisoner, and offers him or her a "deal." If the prisoner confesses, he or she will receive a small sentence. If he or she doesn't confess, and the d.a. wins the case, the d.a. will ask for the maximum sentence. The prisoners also know if that if neither of them confesses there's a good chance that they'll go free. What will each prisoner do? Each knows that if both keep quiet, if they "cooperate" with each other, they may go free. However, neither knows that the other will decide to do that. Both also know that if he or she decides to "defect" and confess, he or she probably will receive a short sentence. But both also know that if they don't confess, and the other does, he or she will receive the maximum sentence. It's to the self-interest of the two to cooperate with each other and not confess, but since neither knows what the other will do, the most rational course is to confess. Consequently, both defect and confess.

This situation can be symbolized by the following "matrix," where:

"c" means to cooperate with the other prisoner and keep silent;

"d" means to defect and confess;

"#1=3" means that for prisoner #1, the

utility of not confessing is 3;
"#2=4" means that for prisoner #2, the utility of defecting is 4, etc.

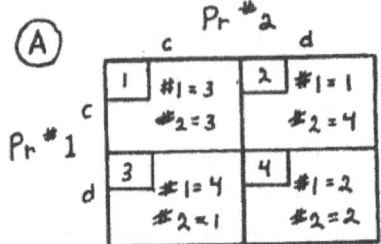

It's evident from this matrix that if both prisoners start in cell #1, they'll be tempted to migrate to cells #2 and #3. If both do this, then both will move next to cell #4.

Many political scientists believe that prisoners' dilemma can be used to symbolize the arms race between the United States and the Soviet Union. They interpret cell #1 as negotiated, multilateral disarmament, cells #2 and #3 as unilateral disarmament for one or the other nation, and cell #4 as continuing the arms race. In cell #4, the utility numbers represent the advantages of political freedom less the costs and dangers of the arms race.

Also, they believe that if pd is played repeatedly, or "iterated" by the same two players, the most effective strategy for each players is "tit-for-tat," for each to make an overture of cooperation, and after that respond in kind. This analysis supports disarmament initiatives and continuing the arms race. Tit-for-tat assumes that the "game" can be played repeatedly for an indefinite period.

Mathematical probability analysis offers insights that alter the character of the game. Since deterrence always has an instantaneous failure probability that can be represented by "p", the probability equation $P = 1 - (1-p)^t$ tells us that, over time (t) the failure probability of deterrence (P) approaches certainty. Since we have no empirical understanding of how long it will be before deterrence collapses into catastrophic nuclear war, the most rational assumption is "worst case," that its collapse is imminent. The imminent collapse of deterrence means that it's irrational to expect that the arms race "game" can be iterated indefinitely. This can be expressed by putting zeros into cell #4 in the game matrix; the utility of a "move" in

which everyone dies can be represented by zero. Mathematical probability analysis therefore makes the game look like this:

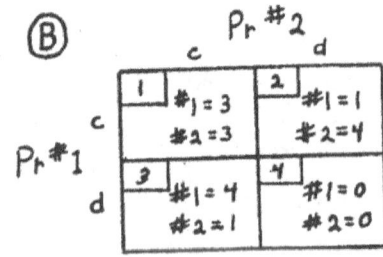

Matrix B isn't prisoners' dilemma. It's the model for a game of bluff called "chicken." In the classical example of chicken, two drivers place their cars on the center line of a highway and speed toward each other. If one swerves before the cars collide, he or she is disgraced and supposedly loses the game.

But the arms race isn't exactly like chicken. While the drivers of the cars can see each other and estimate when they'll crash, we don't know when deterrence will collapse into nuclear war. It's as if the players of chicken couldn't see each other. We can call this game "blind chicken."

Is it rational to play blind chicken? The matrix shows that it isn't. For both "players" in cell #4, the rational choice is to migrate at once to cells 2 and 3, or 1. In all of these cells, the utilities for both "players" are greater than zero.

In this way, rational choice theory, game theory, and mathematical probability analysis combine to show why immediate, unconditional disarmament, and defense by nonviolent resistance – the pacifist policy – is the most scientific and rational course.

---

*   *   *

This article originally was published in the July 12, 1986 edition of the Midwest Pacifist Commentator. To encourage the article's reproduction and distribution, it isn't copyrighted. Additional copies may be obtained from the:

Midwest Pacifist Center
5729 S. Dorchester Ave.
Chicago, IL 60637
Tel: 773-324-0654
Fax: 773-324-6426
Email: blyttle@igc.apc.org

Nuclear War Is Inevitable—Unless...

In terms of mathematic probability, a nuclear war is inevitable and humanity's chances of survival are pitifully small. So contends Prof. Martin Hellman of Stanford University, a brilliant 40-year-old mathematician who is internationally recognized for his expertise in statistics, probability and cryptography.

Hellman's conclusion that nuclear war is inevitable is based on his analysis of facts through a mathematical process called the "two-step Markov principle." Since this reporter readily admitted that Markov's principle was too complicated for him, the good professor explained it in terms of Russian roulette.

Prof. Martin Hellman of Stanford

"In Russian roulette," he began, "you take a revolver with six chambers and load only one. You spin the cylinder, place the barrel against your brain and pull the trigger. There is one chance in six of getting killed. But that's if you play the game only one time. If you play twice, the two chances of being shot reinforce each other, and the odds are almost one in three of killing yourself. After 10 trials, the odds are 84% that you're dead; after 20 trials, 97%. And if you continue to play, the odds become 100% that you will shoot yourself. It's inevitable. In mathematics, we say it happens 'with probability one.' It's certain.

"It doesn't matter if your gun has six chambers or 60 or 600. The smaller probability of killing yourself at each trial prolongs the game, but it does not change the ultimate outcome. You still get shot with probability one."

The professor was then asked to explain simply the analogy of Russian roulette to the inevitability of a nuclear war.

"No one in his right mind," he pointed out, "would play Russian roulette even once. Yet we are continually playing nuclear roulette in which the entire world is at stake. I concede that four decades have elapsed since Hiroshima and Nagasaki without another world war, making people believe nuclear arms are useful in maintaining the peace—that deterrence works. But the real question is not whether nuclear weapons have postponed World War III; the real question is whether they have eliminated its possibility forever. It can only happen once.

"Yet we keep playing nuclear roulette, pulling the trigger more often than most people realize. Every small war is pulling the trigger. Every threat to use violence is pulling the trigger. Every day that goes by in which a missile or a computer can fail is pulling the trigger. Each action in our old-fashioned way of thinking generates another chance of triggering the final global holocaust."

Would a nuclear freeze followed by the gradual destruction of all nuclear weapons prevent the inevitable death of this planet?

"A nuclear freeze," Hellman maintained, "followed by even total disarmament, is not the answer. Our knowledge of how to build nuclear weapons makes disarmament relatively useless. Suppose we outlaw nuclear weapons but don't change our mode of thinking about war in general; my belief is that we may then be more likely to get into a conventional war with the Soviets. Just think that through for a minute. Suppose we engage in a conventional war against the Soviets. The side that is losing will surely be tempted to quickly rebuild nuclear weapons in an effort to save itself.

"I'm convinced the only way to survive nuclear roulette is to stop playing the game, to put down the gun globally, to move beyond war. If we want to avoid the world's imminent suicide, we must shift totally the way we think about war. We no longer can accept it as a means of settling disputes, as an extension of politics or as an innate ingredient in the nature of man."

Appendix 5

Additional copies available from:

Midwest Pacifist Center
5729 S. Dorchester Ave.
Chicago, IL 60637
Tel: 773.324.0654
Fax: 773.324.6426
Email: blyttle@igc.org

www.ingramcontent.com/pod-product-compliance
Lightning Source LLC
Chambersburg PA
CBHW081557280526
45788CB00011B/3495

HARVARD MAGAZINE
July – August 1982
Pp. 18-21

From the Letters section

Nuclear-arms paranoia

My heartfelt thanks to Dr. John E. Mack for his perceptive article, "But what about the Russians?" (March-April, page 21). Many of us are concerned about "nuclear-arms paranoia" and are trying to persuade our leaders to do something about it. We have been stuffed with facts about the dangers of nuclear warfare, but an understanding of the unconscious motives of those who are possessed by this paranoia. along with a gut realization of what such warfare would do to millions of people. can do even more to get us involved. Especially moving were Mack's quotes from concerned teenagers.

ELIZABETH S. HELFMAN, M.A. '34
Southbury, Conn

When Mack finally gets around to the question, ". . . What about the Russians?" he gives non-answers.

He writes: "We are utterly ignorant of each other, of our cultures, histories. and intentions." Is he serious? I am old enough to recall similar nonsense about Hitler's Germany. Wiser heads who suggested reading *Mein Kampf* as an earnest of Nazi intentions were pooh-poohed. Those who urged a hard line against Hitler were called hysterical. Those who saw evil in Fascism and Nazism were said to be believers in a devil theory. Germany, we were told. sees itself ringed by hostile powers. "Once Hitler incorporates the Saar. absorbs the Rhineland, Austria, the Sudeten-Germans . . . Germany will be content."

George Kennan, approvingly quoted by Mack, writes of "the commonality of many of their problems and ours as we both move inexorably into the modern technological age." What common-

ality? Improved gulags? Are we to take Kennan's wishful thinking as a surety of Soviet intentions?

Since the Bolsheviks seized power in 1917, the rulers of the Soviet Union have murdered, conservatively estimated, some sixty million of their own people. How many imprisoned? Six million political prisoners at any one time, Solzhenitsyn estimates. This does not count the dead or imprisoned in the Soviet satellites, in Communist China, Cuba, North Korea, Vietnam, Cambodia, Afghanistan—wherever Communism has ruled. How many witnesses, Dr. Mack, do we need to attest to the character of Soviet culture, history, or intentions?

To fear such a system appears to me profoundly rational. To consider it evil is commonsense. To trust it, foolhardy. To oppose it, morally imperative. It does not help the cause of freedom and peace to paper over Soviet realities. Or to bury our heads in the sand like the ostrich and ignore Soviet intentions.

Ours is a difficult task, and the first priority is to defend the West and its freedoms. Throughout the postwar era, the American deterrent has kept the nuclear peace. Renouncing it now would bring on war. It is the unprecedented Soviet build-up of nuclear and conventional arms that has created the present atmosphere of peril.

It is not "better to be dead than red," it is better to be neither. Sixty million souls surely attest to that. Deterrence is not as pleasant as Mack's illusions, but it will keep us—and Mack—alive and not red.

Pace, Dr. Mack. It is not the "hostility and fear dominating U.S.-Soviet relations and the nuclear proliferation growing out of this fear that most acutely threaten our survival," it is the totalitarian night.

THOMAS R. BROOKS '50
Brooklyn, N.Y.

Many thanks to Mack. I had begun to fear that the subjugation of Eastern Europe and the invasion of Afghanistan were signs that the Soviet Union might really be aggressive after all.

MARK C. BUCHANAN '70
Hyden, Ky.

In his article, Harvard psychiatry professor John E. Mack joins Berkeley professor Michael Nagler in calling for a "paradigm shift" away from aggressiveness and belligerence and toward peace. Students of the social sciences will recall that the idea of a paradigm shift was developed by Thomas S. Kuhn in his 1962 book *The Structure of Scientific Revolutions*. Kuhn's theory is complex, but in essence it is that the scientific understanding of the world progresses by means of sudden shifts

in perspective in which one model or "paradigm" replaces another. An example of this idea offered by the physical sciences is the shift from Newtonian to Einsteinian physics. In the social sciences Marxists have argued that Marxism is a paradigm shift beyond classical economic theory. Under any circumstances, paradigm shifts become possible when scientific research has accumulated enough new information to make possible a theoretical synthesis that is more inclusive than preceding theories, and differs from them in important ways. The appalling dangers to the entire human species inherent in nuclear arsenals and the arms race certainly suggest that a fresh perspective is needed in international relations— one that can avert nuclear war and open up the possibility of unlimited human development. Fortunately, while science has made possible nuclear weapons, it also can suggest the best ways to abolish the weapons and avoid nuclear war.

A key insight is that it's now possible to develop a statistical analysis of strategies for ending the arms race and averting nuclear war. This makes it possible to at least partly remove the evaluation of strategies from the realm of opinion and conjecture, and place it on an objective, scientific footing. For everyone who understands and respects the scientific method, the value in being able to do this is obviously considerable.

To facilitate analysis, we can divide strategies for ending the arms race and avoiding nuclear war into four kinds. The "Establishment" strategy, which has United States and Soviet versions, is to strive for either arms superiority or arms parity, that is, to continue the arms race indefinitely on the assumption that the other side won't be able to keep up. The U.S. version rests on the conjecture that because the Soviet Union has only half the industrial base of the United States, and an inflexible, totalitarian political system, the Soviet Union's economy will be exhausted by the military expenditures exacted by arms competition, and that this will lead to crippling ethnic and nationality conflicts, and perhaps revolution. The Soviet version stems from the theoretical Marxist promise that because of its capitalist character, U.S. society must undergo a socialist revolution generated by class conflict. The parallel between the U.S. and Soviet theories is striking.

Arms control, a second strategy, preserves the principle of "deterrence," but seeks to control the arms race through bilateral agreements verified by inspection. Arms control of the type expressed by the SALT I and SALT II agreements seeks to slow the arms race. "Freeze" arms control seeks to halt the nuclear-arms race at its present arsenal levels. George F. Kennan has proposed halving nuclear arsenals. Key to all arms-control agreements is the inspection, which is designed to eliminate the need for mutual trust.

Unilateral disarmament is a fourth strategy. It can embrace unilateral conventional as well as nuclear disarmament, and also the concept of bilateral disarmament not contingent upon agreements and inspection processes. The strategy of unilateral initiatives has the purpose of generating trust and encouraging an atmosphere of détente through unilateral, reversible disarmament initiatives that don't fundamentally jeopardize the military strength of the nation that undertakes them.

Since the Establishment strategy is dominant, let's examine it first. To prove it unscientific, we must show statistically that the arms race will result in nuclear war.

Under present circumstances, a catastrophic event involving a nuclear weapon could trigger a nuclear war. Such an event might be the launching of a missile. Although one hopes that the leaders of a nation struck by a missile would remain completely rational and cool, it's certainly possible that the sight of one or more of their country's cities or military bases in ruins, and the dead and mutilated bodies of thousands of their countrymen and -women, would stimulate them to make a retaliatory gesture. Such a gesture could easily escalate into all-out war. Let the letter p stand for the chance that any given missile will be launched during a 24-hour period.

We are most interested in the chance of a missile launch over an extended time. An equation that will give this probability to a high degree of accuracy for the values that most interest us and can be understood by anyone with a background in high-school algebra is:

$$AP = 1 - (1 - p)^{n(U+S)}$$

where: AP = The chance of a missile launch over an extended period;
n = The number of days in the period;
U = The number of U.S. missiles; and
S = The number of Soviet missiles.

This equation has two particularly important characteristics. One is that it's an exponential equation that produces a logarithmic curve such as that below. AP approaches certainty over time:

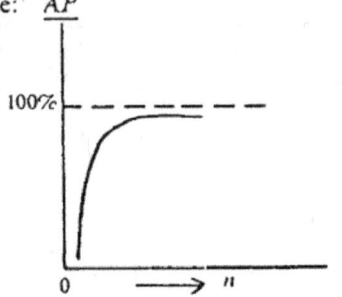

The other is that we immediately have values for all of the variables in the equation except p. We know that $U = 2,000$ (approximately), and $S = 2,000$ (approximately), and that the value of n is a matter of our choice. We can gain some insights into p's value by the exercise of a little imagination and some mathematical experiments.

The value of p must be very small. If it weren't, a missile would have been launched by now, and we'd probably be dead. If we let

$$p = 10^{-7} = \frac{1}{10,000,000} \, ,$$

decide that we want to know what AP will be in ten years ($n = 3,650$), and put all of our values into the equation, we find that AP is equal to about 77%. That value is probably too large. Thousands of missiles have been around for more than ten years, and one hasn't been launched. Therefore, let's try a smaller value for p, say,

$$p = 10^{-8} = \frac{1}{100,000,000} \, .$$

At $p = 10^{-8}$, in ten years, AP equals about 14%. That value is consistent with our being alive. It's therefore reasonable to believe that p's actual value is 10^{-8} or less.

It's possible to learn still more about p's value. For example, a missile might be launched by the failure of some mechanical or electrical component in its launch mechanism. The chance of such a failure could be calculated in much the same way that a team of Massachusetts Institute of Technology scientists under Dr. Norman Rasmussen's direction calculated the chance of a power-reactor accident. Some research along these lines already has been done (see "Too many nuclear weapons," September-October, page 17).

Also, a missile might be launched because of the psychological breakdown of its launching crew. Here, too, relevant research already has been done into the psychological stability of the personnel who control nuclear weapons. Calculation of these probabilities could provide a minimum, or base value, for p. The chance of other possible causes of a missile launch, such as a decision by a strategic-weapons command center, a national leader, or a terrorist group, would be more difficult to quantify and calculate, but could be added to the base value. The value of p would become greater in times of international crisis.

Still other insights provided by the equation are that the more missiles there are, the higher is the likelihood of war, and that although p may be astronomically small, over a period of only a few years, the chance of war can become alarmingly high. It's obvious that p's value is of great importance to

the human species. Governments should be required to make public all information that could bear upon the calculation of p.

Once we realize that we actually can calculate the probability of a missile launch—the outbreak of nuclear war—the Establishment strategy, be it the U.S. or Soviet version, is no longer rational. It represents the assumption that speculations have a higher degree of probability than the logarithmic curve of the equation. There's no way to quantify the conjectures of U.S. or Soviet strategists concerning the probability of a collapse of each other's cultures for economic or political reasons. On the other hand, it is possible to calculate the probability of the outbreak of nuclear war. To base policy on conjecture rather than on statistical projection is unscientific.

In addition, the probability equation shows that the leaders of the U.S. and Soviet Union are playing a lethal global game with the human species similar to Russian roulette. In Russian roulette, the players put one bullet into the chamber of a revolver, then in turn take up the weapon, spin the chamber, place the muzzle to their heads, and pull the trigger. In U.S. - Soviet roulette, H-bombs are the bullet, missiles the revolver, the players point the weapon at each other, and everyone can be killed when the gun finally goes off. Also, the players keep putting more bullets into the chamber, which increases the chance of the gun firing.

The equation provides still another insight about the Establishment strategy: A national leader who claims that he or she can at once maintain a strong nuclear deterrent and preserve peace is either unaware of the character of modern strategic weapons systems, or is deceiving us.

Of the remaining three strategies, unilateral initiatives are probably unable to stop the arms race. Any reversible disarmament step will appear to be a deception, a ruse, and won't generate trust. No genuine disarmament step is likely to result from this strategy.

Of the two remaining strategies, SALT-type arms control can slow but not stop the arms race. Arms control will increase the period within which nuclear war will become probable. Freeze arms control will lock nations into the present values of the equation. That will further increase the period within which nuclear war will become probable but won't prevent nuclear war. Both SALT-type and freeze arms control continue the game of roulette, but at somewhat less risky levels than the Establishment strategy.

As arms control proceeds and reduces nuclear-weapons levels, it can steadily increase the odds of the roulette game. Arms control's main difficulty lies with inspection. The SALT treaties have shown how difficult and time consuming it is to establish satisfactory verification of agreements. Freeze advocates claim that inspection of freeze agreements would work because large missile and bomber bases, and missile and bomber production and assembly facilities, can be monitored by satellites, and that there are so many nuclear weapons that minor treaty violations won't matter. This suggests that arms control will work only at levels of nuclear arms about equal to present ones, and that's inadequate for preventing nuclear war. The difficulty of developing satisfactory inspection procedures for lower levels of nuclear weapons can be understood by recalling that nuclear weapons can now be made so compact that hundreds will fit into a small room, only a few weapons are needed to give military superiority over conventional arsenals, the U.S. and the Soviet Union have tens of thousands of weapons, and bombs can be delivered by many means other than large missiles, such as cruise missiles, submarines, disguised boats, disguised airplanes, and even trucks, automobiles, and large suitcases. The temptation for a nation engaged in arms control to hide a cache of weapons would be enormous, and no way of preventing this from happening seems available.

Despite arms control's difficulties, freeze agreements followed by attempts to reduce arms levels are plainly more rational and scientific than the Establishment's strategy.

Unilateral disarmament would immediately reduce many of the values in the probability equation by about half and therefore make war less likely. It's unlikely that a nation engaging in unilateral nuclear disarmament would suffer a nuclear attack. First-strike attacks are made probable by the increasing armaments of an "enemy," not by decreasing armaments. The present fears about a "window of vulnerability," and

the Japanese attack on Pearl Harbor, which was designed to halt the growing power of the U.S. Pacific Fleet and Air Force, are examples of this principle. A nation with nuclear arms would have strong reasons *not* to attack a nation that was disarming. An attack would poison the ecosphere shared by everyone, risk a retaliatory attack, destroy valuable human and other resources, and wreak great damage to the attacking nation's global political image. Since nuclear weapons are inherently dangerous and costly, the rational response to unilateral disarmament would be to quickly reduce one's own arsenals of nuclear weapons.

Thus, unilateral nuclear disarmament probably would greatly decrease the likelihood of nuclear war.

A nation engaging in unilateral nuclear disarmament would have good reasons to reduce its conventional arms as well. Conventional arms are no match for nuclear arms, and their use against an enemy armed with nuclear weapons would invite a nuclear attack, as the bombings of Hiroshima and Nagasaki show. Furthermore, conventional weapons are expensive and contribute to inflation.

The principles that make unilateral disarmament an effective way to end the arms race between the U.S. and the Soviet Union, and to prevent nuclear war, would apply to arms races between other nations—for example, to the arms race between the Soviet Union and China.

Any nation that practiced unilateral disarmament would be wise to pursue nonmilitary alternatives for defending its values and institutions. Massive economic-aid programs to combat poverty and other causes of cynicism, desperation, and aggression; the development of global institutions that would promote political freedom and economic justice; and preparation for nonviolent resistance to cope with the possibility of invasion and occupation are examples of alternatives.

International relations conducted in such a manner might or might not be expressions of a new paradigm. Certainly, they would be more rational and scientific than the strategies based on conjectures now being followed by the superpowers, which can be shown by statistical analysis to be propelling the world toward nuclear war.

BRADFORD LYTTLE
Chicago

Additional copies available from the:

MIDWEST PACIFIST CENTER
5729 S. Dorchester Ave.
Chicago, IL 60637
Tel: 773-324-0654
Fax: 773-324-6426
Email: blyttle@igc.apc.org

Appendix 2

The Enola Gay and the Apocalypse Equation

$$AP = 1-(1-p)^{Txn}$$

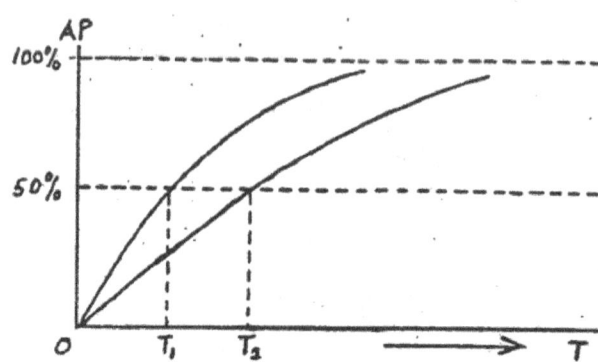

The Enola Gay was the first plane to drop an atomic bomb on a city. Why the bomb was dropped is a matter of dispute. A popular view is that Hiroshima and Nagasaki were atom bombed to end the war against Japan as quickly as possible. Many critics of the atomic bombings argue, with substantial evidence, that the main motive for the bombings was to intimidate the Soviet Union. Regardless of why the bombs were dropped two facts are indisputable:

First, the bombings violated the moral principles of Christianity and all of the world's major humanitarian religions and philosophies. In this, they were similar to most acts of war.

Second, the bombings introduced atomic weapons to warfare. Atomic weapons are different from conventional weapons in that they are much more "efficient"; that is, they are much more powerful, and much easier to deliver. It took thousands of bombers and the lives of 150,000 Allied airmen to destroy Germany's cities. One plane and one bomb destroyed Hiroshima. None of the Enola Gay's crew was even injured. Today, a strategic nuclear missile can carry as many as ten warheads, each with an explosive power at least ten times the power of the bomb that destroyed Hiroshima, and deliver these warheads with pinpoint accuracy. Thermonuclear bombs also can be delivered clandestinely. There is no defense against these weapons.

The nuclear arms race developed because national "leaders" believed that a strategy existed that would permit nuclear weapons to be instruments for preserving "peace," without being dropped on an "enemy" in anger. This strategy, "nuclear deterrence," is the foundation of United States foreign policy. Deterrence is based on the reasoning that if an "enemy" can be convinced that a nuclear attack will result in such devastating retaliation that the consequences of the attack will be a net loss, the attack will never occur. Also, one of the main principles of deterrence strategy is that a nation should have a large number of well protected nuclear missiles. Such an arsenal will be difficult to destroy in a "first strike" attack.

What is wrong with nuclear deterrence? It can be criticized on moral grounds. It is wrong to threaten to kill millions of people in an act of retaliation. Beyond that, in the long run it will not work. It will lead to thermonuclear war. The Apocalypse Equation (AE) shows why.

The AE shows how the probability of a nuclear missile launch is related to time. Deterrence strategy ignores time. It is based on static speculations about the psychological effects of nuclear weapons. But time is crucial to the development of probability. This is understood in the natural sciences and industry, such as physics, chemistry, biology, genetics, and the insurance industry. These fields often use equations that show probability is related to time. Such equations are called

(please turn over)